13th Nov. 2020

To Joyce

What Is LifeWithout My Love?

n each
60 years!
even possible!!
we are still enjoying
"The goodness of the Lord
in the land of the living"
(Psalm 27:13)
And its not over yet!!.

IAN JENNINGS

Love and Blessings

IAN
xx

Copyright © 2020 Rev Ian Jennings

All rights reserved.

No part of this book may be reproduced or distributed in any form or by any means, including photocopying, without written permission of the author, except in the case of brief quotations embodied in reviews.

ISBN: 9798555820808

Dedicated to the memory of my wife, Barbara, with whom it was as easy to stay in love as it was to fall in love.

REVIEWS

For those who are journeying through grief I have always recommended "A Grief Observed" by C. S. Lewis and now I have found a worthy companion volume, equally moving yet so different.

Ian has given us something simple yet profound. He does not dwell overmuch on his own journey of grief but shares those of others in simple stories. He takes us through the various ups and downs of what is for most people a long and sometimes painful time.

He asks the deep and difficult questions but does not offer simplistic answers. He gives hope to those who may be bordering on despair. Ian speaks from a deeply Christian heart but includes those with little or no faith.
This is a faithful companion by one who is undertaking and sharing it with integrity, love and not a little courage. Thank you, Ian.

The Rt Reverend Jack Nicholls
Former Bishop of Sheffield.

I have known Ian for 50 years, as a friend and colleague. He was always a 'wordsmith' brilliantly crafting his sermons and now adapting his skills in a new sphere as an author. This book is brilliant and helpful, it is full of poignant memories which provide the basis for approaching the matter of bereavement.

Dealing with grief and its impact are covered in both biblical and practical ways. The advice carries the compassion of Jesus as Ian draws on his own journey "through the valley of the shadow of death."

For those of us who knew Ian before he was married to Barbs, and watched their delightful and romantic marriage, this book carries authority because they enjoyed an authentic relationship rooted in love for one another.

They never lost the romance from their lives and so this book carries weight as an important contribution to the issue of facing the future and the inevitability of loss.

I think this book is going to be a major support to many. Ian's first book, *By a Departing Light* was quite "raw" and I shed many tears ... This one has powerful insights into the emotion and feelings that accompany bereavement but is more practical and I'm sure will provide counsel for many.

Peter Butt
Director of School of Ministries Leadership Training Programme.

This book is brilliant, readable, informative and so very practical. It is a great resource for those of us who try to help people who are dealing with the death of a loved one. I feel it would be an invaluable tool for a support group too. It is also a book to have on hand as one day it may be really needed personally. In this book Ian turns his own heart ache into a huge positive for others.

Roger Blackmore
Founder and Lead Pastor of Genesis Church, Long Island, New York.

The combination of Ian's own journey of bereavement and his insights as a Pastor have produced a really valuable book for those who are facing the loss of a loved one, and for those who are seeking to help them. Stories of family members, friends and congregants are interspersed with encouragement that is both helpful and sensitive. At times I found myself with a tear in my eye, at other times I was smiling. This is one of those books I am really glad I read.

David Jones
Lead Pastor - City Church, (Great Grimsby and North East Lincs.)

In his book – **"What is life without my love?"** Ian continues to explore grief – especially the loss of a spouse. The strength of this book is not just Ian's deep Christian faith which has sustained him throughout but also the way in which he openly shares his own experience of grief and that of family, friends and colleagues.

For those who are devastated by the loss of someone close – be it a spouse, parent, sibling or child, this book will reassure, comfort and sometimes challenge.

Of all the views shared, the overriding and very positive message is one of gratitude; gratitude for the lives we have shared with our loved ones.

Ian's love for Barbara shines through as he bravely tells of the last eighteen months of her life. On his personal journey of grief Ian tells us that there is a choice to be made and hard though it will be, choosing, *"the spiritual discipline of focusing our minds upon God and our thoughts on memories that enrich rather than undermine"* is a powerful, positive message fore anyone posing the same question – *"What is life without my love?"*

Sue Mellor, (Headteacher, Aston, All Saints C of E Junior and Infants School.)

Simple yet profound, clear-headed yet deeply passionate, Ian Jennings's second book reflects beautifully on the challenge of losing a spouse and offers solid, practical and biblical guidance for confronting grief. 'What is Life Without My Love?' tells the story of a wide variety of people who have faced such loss, highlighting lessons they have learned and how their dark experience can be a source of light to others following the same path.

This book will be a great consolation to many facing personal tragedy.

Dr Andrew Davies, Director, The Edward Cadbury Centre of the Public Understanding of Religion.

CONTENTS

	Acknowledgments	i
1	Mortality	5
2	The Precipice	14
3	The Heart that is Broken is the Heart that is Open	21
4	Left Behind	30
5	Signs of Life, Signs of Love	36
6	Release, Relief, Regret	44
7	Planning Not Drifting	52
8	Anniversaries and Special Dates	60
9	Children: The Gift That Keeps on Giving	69
10	The Place of Pilgrimage	78
11	A Change of Identity	86
12	Grief in a Time of Isolation	94
13	Gone Too Soon	104
14	Home	114
	About The Author	123

ACKNOWLEDGMENTS

You will find many names mentioned in the pages of this book, all of them who have been a great help in enabling me to write a book with a depth of insight and practical advice. I have so much appreciated conversations that were deep, honest and very moving. Thank you, Fay Williams, Joan Craven, Deloris Smith, Trish Watt, Antony Graham, Jeff Elliott, Lynnette Burton, Hazel de Quervain and Michael Clarke whose conversations have been both heart wrenching and heart-warming but above all deeply inspiring.

Also, I am grateful to Barry Baxter my old school friend for his depiction of 'our tree' in acrylics - the front cover of this book.

I am indebted to Jude Cole for her proof-reading skills.

FOREWORD

Ian Jennings is a man with a passion and a fund of helpful advice coming straight out of his personal experience. Born of his own struggles following the death of his wife, her writes especially for those who find themselves in a similar situation, with all the sensitivity of someone who has been there and understands what it is like. He avoids the temptation to give easy answers to hard questions, and although he is well informed on what experts have to say about bereavement, he is never academic or detached.

On the contrary he writes in the sort of style that makes it easy to imagine that you are sitting in a personal conversation with someone who really does know and empathize with how you might be feeling at a time of great grief and tragedy.

As a minister he has spent a lifetime caring for others, but this is far removed from a book of professional advice, be sure, it is full of stories drawn from a lifetime's engagement with people at times of crisis, but it also honest and open about the authors own feelings – not in a self-indulgent way, but through an interweaving of scripture and personal reflection it will bring hope to many, and inspiration to those who may be supporting the recently bereaved.

There is no shortage of practical suggestions for living through grief, but above all it is a book that acknowledges painful realities while pointing to new possibilities, all of it grounded in Christian faith.

For those who are working through the loss of a loved

one, this will bring comfort and inspiration, but those who are supporting others through bereavement will also find benefits from Ian's insights into the reality that they are facing and though written primarily for individuals it would also be an ideal resource for a death café or bereavement group.

John Drane

John Drane is the author of The Macdonaldisation of the Church (Darton Longman and Todd 2000) Do Christians know how to be Spiritual? (Darton Longman and Todd 2005) as well as 3 best-selling books on the Bible that have been translated into 60 languages. For more than 20 years he has played a key role in ecumenical thinking on action on mission – Co-Chair of the Mission Theology Advisory Group of the Archbishops Council of the Church of England.

AUTHOR'S INTRODUCTION

When I finished writing *By a Departing Light (growing through grief)* I felt there was more to be said. I really didn't want to write a second book on the subject of processing grief but I learned so much from conversations and feed- back from readers that the second book demanded to be written.

I also felt that this book could serve as a resource for church-based bereavement groups as well as helpful to individual readers. This book is essentially about a Christian approach to grief and so many churches run bereavement groups and I hope that this book will bring some helpful input to such groups.

I attended a bereavement group following the death of my wife. It was an opportunity to sit and talk to others in a similar situation but it was entirely 'self help' and there was no input whatsoever. Many expressed the thought that though the group was a great help it would have been appreciated if there had been, at least, some minimal enabling of focus. I think this book could help with that.

If each member of the group were to read an agreed chapter before attending, that could serve the purpose of focusing hearts and minds and the questions and reflection at the end of each chapter will help with that process.

Ian Jennings

1

MORTALITY

When I was 12 years old my parents bought our first gramophone; it was bulky, brown and Bakelite. I rushed home from school ready to be entertained. The excitement soon subsided however, because my parents had invested in only two records, neither of which set my pulse racing. They were Paul Robeson singing, 'Swing Low Sweet Chariot' and Kathleen Ferrier singing, 'What is Life to be with Thee - what is Life without my Love?' These were clearly not chosen with the tastes of a 12-year-old boy in mind. Our record collection was, however, very slow to build, so I listened to Paul Robson and Kathleen Ferrier ad infinitum. My pals were listening to Elvis Presley and Lonnie Donegan while my ears were pinned to Robson and Ferrier – never a conversation for the playground! Despite it all, I came to appreciate those richly beautiful voices and the songs are strangely memorable; hence the title of this book – "What is Life without my Love?"

In the song the question is rhetorical; a plaintive cry of deep sadness. For the purposes of this book it is a question which needs to be answered; a real question – what is life following the death of a spouse? What purposes do, constraints, challenges, value, hopes and destiny still play? That is the question this book attempts to investigate.

My Grandson, Jamie was 5 when one day he suddenly said to me, "Grandpa I wish I had a mouse that wouldn't die!"

I said, "Do you mean the mouse would be your friend forever and would never leave you?"

"Yes," he responded, "that would be so cool." (Even at 5 he was into 'cool.') "But they do all die don't they?" he mused. Then, after a quiet moment of thoughtfulness he added, "Grandpa, will I die?" This was a question I was reluctant to answer but I responded gently, "Well, yes Jamie. But you don't need to worry about that at all because it won't happen until you're very old." Quick as thought, he looked up at me and replied, "But Grandpa, you're already very old!" I had been trying to divert his attention away from his own mortality, but his winsome naivety he was fixing my attention on my own!

I love the way that children, in all innocence, get straight to the heart of the matter.

I believe many of us cope with our mortality by avoiding thoughts of our own death. I have heard it said, 'death is the one event which seems most natural when related to others, but most unnatural when related to ourselves.' That is part of the human psyche. Sasha Baron Cohen's satirically fictional character Ali Gee purported to be at the cutting edge of youth culture. He conducted outrageous interviews with well-known figures who didn't realise initially that it was spoof. In one show he quizzed a scientist about medical breakthroughs. The scientist remarked, 'Of course we can prolong life only so far; everyone dies eventually."

"Not me," responded Ali Gee with his characteristic brash confidence. The scientist looked bemused, "No really," he said, "There are no exceptions, everyone will die."

"Well I ain't gonna die for sure," replied Ali Gee. The scientist's face was a picture, thinking he was speaking to a super-charged, intellectually-challenged, celebrity belonging to youth culture, who really believed he was exempt from death. Though we generally don't exhibit a similar rejection of our own death, at some level we may well be in a state of denial.

Death often used to be called 'the last taboo.' We live in a society that is disinhibited about almost everything except death. But maybe there is some evidence of change and a greater willingness to talk about death. In 2019 BBC Radio 4 aired a programme called, 'We Need to Talk About Death.' At the same time the award-winning comedian, Angela Barnes was presenting a series on Radio 4 in which she made death the main subject of her comedy; focusing on the death of her Father in off-beat comedic narratives. If this last taboo becomes the focus of humour perhaps it will demystify death without trivialising it. Maybe we are becoming more ready for realistic conversations about death as natural part of life, just as birth is; commencement and conclusion - both parts of our journey. Thirty months after my wife's death I was reluctantly sorting through family papers and found Barbara's birth certificate. Shuffling my way through more papers, I found her death certificate. I took a paper clip and fastened them together. A poignant and painful moment, it prompted me to write these lines;

Sorting Papers.

WHAT IS LIFE WITHOUT MY LOVE?

Amongst mundane receipts, reminders and records
An Alpha and Omega of sombre documents
Bearing the dear name, 'Barbara Ruth Jennings.'
I pin them together; a birth certificate and death certificate.

A heavy-hearted act of bleak completion;
Two papers spanning 65 years
Now together in the same box file.
65 years between two single pages,
65 years of laughter, love and learning,
Full years – good years.

Now not a breath between them
A flimsy duo clipped together.

My world in a pink paper clip.

It was another moment of being ambushed by grief. Life's beginning and ending are perfectly acceptable as objective facts, but it is quite a different story when you are living through the experience. Often it is not our own mortality which causes most angst, if we are in an interdependent and deeply loving relationship it is the mortality of the other which cause us the worst anxiety in our pensive moments.

A happy marriage is a gift beyond price. St Peter speaks of marriage partners as being, " Heirs together of the grace of life.' In other words, partners into whose hands the gift of life has been entrusted to be shared, valued, celebrated and nurtured. It is a vivid picture of successful marriage and although a marriage may not begin there, with careful nurture and mutual care and commitment, it may grow there.

I used to be the Rector of a very active and lively parish, at its heart an extraordinarily beautiful 12th century church. The gate at the rear of its churchyard led into the grounds of an hotel which had been the Manor House in earlier centuries and now it is a popular wedding reception venue. Consequently, our parish church was an attractive prospect for weddings. In some years I conducted 60 weddings - in an era when weddings in Church were in decline. In order to prepare the happy couples, I would hold two major gatherings with up to 30 couples in each. In the course of my talk I would say, "I'm sure you will have read that one in three marriages end in divorce. I just want to point out that there are thirty couples here this evening which means that 10 of you are not going to make it! Your marriage will end in the divorce court, maybe with bitterness, betrayal and acrimony!" It wasn't a speech they were expecting to hear at a marriage preparation evening. I would pause to let the words sink in and would observe the look of incomprehension on their faces as they leaned over and whispered something to each other. It was a dramatic moment! I knew they were saying to each other, "Well that's not going to be us – we're going the distance," or words to that effect. I liked that moment because it was my cue to suggest strategies promoting a beautifully creative and successful marriage relationship, 'till death us do part.'

There is a beautiful scene between father and daughter in Captain Corelli's Mandolin by Louis de Bernieres. On the eve of his daughter's wedding Dr Iannis says to his daughter, 'Love is a temporary madness, it erupts like volcanos and then subsides. And when it subsides you have to make a decision. You have to work out whether your root was so entwined together that it is inconceivable that you should ever part. Because this is what love is. Love is not breathlessness, it is not excitement, it is not the promulgation of promises of eternal passion. That is just being in love, which any fool can do. Love itself is what is left over when being in love has burned away and this is both an art and a fortunate accident. Your Mother and I had it, we had roots that grew towards each other underground, and when all the pretty blossom had fallen from our branches we found that we were one tree and not two.' It is not just a beautiful speech, but the realistic description of a beautiful marriage.

In my work as a Pastor I have to admit not all marriages are like that but nonetheless along the ups and downs of life's road, some couples work out a way of being which is enriching; not perfect but really worthwhile. Of course, some marriages can be a disaster. The preacher, John Wesley had a marriage which was far from successful. On one occasion a young man asked Wesley should he ask a particular young woman to marry him. Wesley expressed serious doubts on the basis of what he knew about the couple. The young man claimed, 'But she is a fine Christian!' Wesley is said to have commented, 'Well, God can live with people who you and I would find impossible to live with!' Some relationships are never meant to be.

My friend, a Hospital Chaplain, was sitting at the bedside of a dying man and the man's wife was sitting at the other side of the bed. She solemnly shook her head and slowly said, "60 years! 60 years!"
My friend said, "Oh is that how long you have been married?" She sighed a long slow sigh replying' "Yes, 60 years married." My friend responded by saying, "Oh how wonderful!" She said, emphatically, "No! It's been bloody awful!" As I said, some marriages are not meant to be. No

one signs up for a lifetime of misery and yet, of course, sometimes that is the sad outcome. We would be naïve to assume every marriage is an "Heirs together of the grace of life" experience. And we would be cruel to expect couples who have no shared joy and a life devoid of mutual flourishing to stay together through a bitter, baleful journey.

In this book I am addressing those for whom the loss of their spouse is a painful prospect which, at times, brings them to the edge of desperation. The death of my wife inspired me to write a book called 'By a Departing Light.' Indeed, when we knew that Barbara's condition was terminal she had said to me, "you should write a book about this." I'm sure she felt it would be good therapy for me and I wondered if it might be helpful for others on the same journey of loss. Many friends encouraged me to write it while some found they couldn't read it because it raised too many distressing issues about mortality, especially that of their loved one. The question hovered in the air, 'What is life without my love?'

My friend Barry was Head Boy in the Cathedral School where I was also a pupil. He was known for his irrepressible cheerfulness and sterling integrity. He still is- but now he is in his early 70s. After the publication of my book he sent me the following message, "Hi Ian, I've read all your posts about your lovely wife and have often thought you should write a book. However, now that you have I am frightened to death to read it. I'm so very frightened of the prospect of being without my Sue if she predeceased me... I find it very difficult even to think about."

When we were young my wife and I sometimes talked about death. I remember strolling hand in hand on a cliff top pathway, one glorious summer day; we were in reflective mood and each of us tried to imagine life without the other. We were very much in love and agreed that to be in this world without each other was inconceivable. We decided our ideal vision of our last day on earth would be to die within minutes of one another, our funeral would be a double event and we would enter eternal rest together. It was a very romantic notion. On only one occasion have I witnessed something akin to this; our good friends Phillip and Jean Woofindin. Both had become increasingly ill and the question of how either one would survive without the other was worrying both for them and their children. In the event, Jean predeceased Phillip by only a few days. Their funeral service was a celebration of their shared lives. It had a wonderful sense of completion. Their son, Mark put together the service booklet, in which he included a beautiful photograph of them laughing together. They were enjoying one another's company and laughing together, perfectly captured in the photo. It seemed so appropriate, at the completion of their life's journey together, that their coffins should lie side by side at the front on the church. Neither had had to address the question, "What is life without my love?"

But most of us do have to address the question and it is a very unwelcome prospect – a heart-sinking vision of the future, perhaps too difficult to contemplate, yet, for most of us, it is inevitable.

For Reflection

Psalm 90: 10 ***The days of our life are three score years and ten and if by reason of strength they be four score*** *years, yet is their strength labour and sorrow.* That is not a hugely encouraging text if, like me, you have already passed the seventy milestone. Perhaps it needs to be balanced with scriptures like Psalm 92: 14 *In old age they will still bear fruit; healthy and green they will remain.* I must admit to preferring that text. However, the question remains, have we fully bought into the idea of completing the race; finishing the course and dying well.

Psalm 90: 12 reads, *So teach us to number our days that we may apply our hearts to wisdom.*

Have we done that? Not as a mathematical exercise but as a reflective experience.

Coming to terms with the death of a life partner is not the work of a moment; it takes times. But remember that *the Lord sustains the Fatherless and the widow. He heals the broken hearted and binds up their wounds* (Psalm 147: 3)

The Lord is your constant companion on this journey of loss.

2

THE PRECIPICE

When your spouse dies, by sudden death or by life sapping disease, it is like stepping off a precipice. There is no safety net; merely a void beneath your feet and you - in free fall. That is how it feels. The sense of loss and pain of grief is all consuming.

Fay confided in her husband, Keith, that she was anxious about the future when all their children would have left home and established their own independent lives. Their youngest son was in the military, recently married and been posted abroad. 'What now?' was the question which tormented her mind and she was feeling a little redundant and anxious. He was very reassuring. "This is our time ", he said with a broad warm smile. "We have raised our kids to be masters of their own lives, now we get our independence and can do things we have never had time to do. I'm retiring – it's going to be great! This is our time.'

Fay took his words to heart, was reassured and began to

look forwards. A few days later, they had just enjoyed after-dinner coffee. He took the cups back to the kitchen; returned to the sitting room and sat down. He sighed. That was his last breath.

Fay's world fell apart; she told me she wanted to die. For two years she longed to join him and yearned for the embrace of death. Adjustment to her loss came slowly, however, piece by piece she eventually constructed a new life into which she carried the nurturing memories of the love of her life. As Fay discovered, a sudden and wholly unexpected death is particularly bewildering and devastating.

What she and so many others experience, was a deep sense of anguish. The tectonic plates of her life had not only shifted, but collapsed. That's how it feels for so many and the crushing anguish can't be avoided: it is the profundity of deep grief.

It can be mitigated to a degree through a loving family and caring friends. If deep anguish were not eased it would overwhelm the mourner. Anguish, derived from the Latin word *angustiae,* meaning extreme pain. A feeling of suffering is typically preceded by a tragedy or an event which has profound meaning, suffering which is mental, emotional and physical. Grief has all those elements – mental anguish; physical ache in the hollow of the chest and emotional suffering and distress. The question, 'What is life without my love?' – would elicit the answer, 'there is no life without my love.' That is when anguish is in danger of becoming despair.

In reality, however, anguish often gives way to anger in the early stages of grief. Anger is part of our human condition, a sense of outrage at the desperate unfairness of life. Often anger is unfocused. It is wide sweeping rage against the universe; or against God. It may also be against the loved one who had the temerity to leave this life. There is no logic in this anger. A grief-stricken spouse knows their loved one did not choose to exit this world and leave them alone, but who else deserves the anger? Some rage at God and it is right to do so - He understands. No human companion can understand more deeply than the God who is Love.

A friend who is a minister in the Methodist Church once told me of a member of his church whose wife had cancer. He was visiting her daily in the hospital. She was very ill, but he continued to hope and pray for her recovery. He formed a habit of popping into a nearby church on his way to the Hospital to say a prayer for his wife. On the day of her birthday he was taking a birthday cake on the visit with him. That morning, the ward sister rang with good news; the patient was improving. It seems she was responding well to treatment and the sister wanted to pass on this good news before he visited that day. He was overjoyed.

As usual, he popped into the church on his way to hospital; this time to thank God for this good news. When he arrived at the Ward the Sister greeted him, solemn faced and asked him to step into the office. "I'm so sorry to tell you, but after my call to you today your wife took a sudden, wholly unexpected turn for the worse. She died a few minutes before you arrived. I'm so sorry."

The news seemed all the more brutal because his hopes had been raised that morning. The light of hope had shone brightly and briefly only to be completely extinguished. He felt anguish and desperation but he also felt very angry with God. That she should die on her birthday seemed painfully poignant.

Later, when he left the Hospital, he remembered he had left the cake in the church. He had placed it on the pew beside him when he had popped in to offer his prayer of thanksgiving and in his haste to see the improvement in his wife, he had forgotten it. On his way home, he went into the church once more to pick up the cake. He looked up at the crucifix hanging above the altar and he seethed with anger against God. A swift, irresistible surge of rage swept over him and he launched the cake towards the crucifix, where it smashed into a thousand pieces covering the altar and the sanctuary. Feeling a sudden release, he turned on his heels and left the church.

Later, as my friend, the Methodist Minister sat with him to discuss funeral arrangements, he confided what he had done with the cake, now feeling guilt and regret. My friend reassured him, saying, "You did exactly the right thing; in throwing the cake you cast your anger, grief and heartache upon God. Remember what Isaiah says, 'He bore our grief and carried our sorrows,' he did that on the cross. You literally hurled your anger and distress at the cross! Good - the cross is not only the best place, but the only place for it.'

It was a dramatic and vivid metaphor for grief but also a beautiful embodiment of grace.

The lasting legacy of anguish and anger is anxiety. By that I mean a lingering, persistent state of worry and vulnerability. Everything has changed forever. Your love is gone; whichever way you try to rearrange events in your mind, nothing now can alter one grim fact - you come home to an empty house.

Following my wife's death there were times in the middle of a busy day when something would happen which stirred my imagination and a familiar thought would arise, "I can't wait to tell Barbara about this." Then fast on the heels of that thought another, unwelcome one would intrude, "You can't, you never will."

That finality can leave you with a permanent sense of anxiety, one to which there is no easy solution. It has to do with mortality and vulnerability. With each new day that same anxiety returns with the ever-present question to which there is no satisfactory answer, 'What is life without my love?'

I spoke to a friend whose husband had died 18 years before who had developed a clear understanding of this persistent anxiety. She is one of the liveliest people you could meet, but in spite of her capacity to embrace life, she recognises that both for her daughter and herself there has been an underlying anxiety and an awareness of vulnerability at all times, a thin mist which makes the sun less bright. Living with loss introduces that subtle anxiety. Life can no longer be trusted: things fall apart. My friend lives life to the full; values each day; cherishes life's great gifts and yet, at the heart of things, anxiety remains.

When couples are young and in love they will often weave a narrative for themselves which becomes their own. Of course, it never includes the early death of one partner so when it happens, it is deeply shocking. It seems a broken promise, a brutal betrayal but there is no one, and nothing on whom to pin the blame.

Trish, whose husband died of pancreatic cancer, was

devastated by his swiftly moving illness and death. She read my book, 'By a Departing Light' in an effort to find some help in her grief. She had been used to going on holiday with her oldest friend, Chris, the friend who had introduced her to Bill when they were all young. He would smilingly wave them off on their trip and then get back to working or pursuing a cherished project. Four months after Bill's death, she and her friend decided to fly off to the sunshine. It seemed like a good idea and Trish felt a rest and time in the sun with her best friend would help her grief. The night she and her friend arrived in Tenerife she felt very low. She messaged me saying, 'I'm overwhelmed with heartache. I left our home this morning and for the first time Bill didn't wave me off. I need you to tell me this gets easier.'

When she got back from Tenerife she wrote, 'While the weather was beautiful and the sun helped my aching body, nothing can help my heartache. I found it unbelievably difficult seeing couples happily enjoying their holiday and knowing I'll never have that again. I get lots of hugs from my sons and grandchildren but the hardest thing was the realisation that I will never hold hands again …we always held hands and it something I will miss forever."

When anguish subsides and anger settles the persistent anxiety and vulnerability remain. Life will never be the same again, but the base metal of anxiety can be transmuted into the pure gold of loving action.

What is life without my love?

Anguish? - Anger? - Anxiety?

Most probably - but light, life, and hope beckon us on to a worthwhile future.

For Reflection

Psalm 27 : 13 The Psalmist writes, ***I would have fainted unless I had believed to see the goodness of the Lord in the land of the living.***

That feeling of fainting – losing energy; losing heart and losing purpose is present in the hearts of those who grieve.

How can you see the goodness of the Lord in the land of the living? Is it still identifiable in the light of all that you have been through?

'Faith and Fainting' are both mentioned here by the Psalmist. How can faith counter fainting?

Is the 'Goodness of the Lord' part of your present experience?

Do you expect to see more of the goodness of the Lord in the future? How?

3

THE HEART THAT IS BROKEN IS THE HEART THAT IS OPEN

Grief can either turn inwards in bleak devastation or outwards in redemptive action. There is always a period of devastation in which the question 'What is life without my love?' leads the grieving heart into unmitigated sorrow. Living with that reality for a period is inevitable. How long this darkest period lasts depends on the individual; everyone's experience is different. But the flip side of vulnerability is sensitivity; the experience of loss can open the heart to a new awareness of the pain of others.

One of the lovely things I observed while attending St. Luke's Bereavement Group in Sheffield, was how the community of loss became a community of care. Most of the those attending the fortnightly Tuesday morning group had lost their spouse whilst they were experiencing 'end of life' care at St Luke's Hospice. The group was run without any leadership input; it was essentially a group of people sitting in a room for a couple of hours drinking tea and coffee and talking to one another.

It had been grief that brought them together but it was care which held them together. That was certainly true of the group with whom I was immediately involved. What began as a fortnightly group, developed into something truly rewarding - people began to watch out for one another and to pick up on one another's darker moments. Words of encouragement were given, phone calls made, impromptu meetings happened. I was struck by the degree of sensitivity and empathy which they had one for another. It became a pastoral community that was safe, accepting and deeply caring.

A disparate group of people with little in common, except for their shared pain of loss, made the serendipitous discovery of the depth of their own humanity. Each one's own vulnerability seemed to deepen their sensitivity which in turn led to compassionate action towards others. A broken heart is an open heart - it is sad indeed when grief becomes permanently turned inwards so devastation becomes the only reality.

Fay, who I mentioned earlier seemed, initially to fall into this category. For two years she longed to die: had no hope; saw no future; entertained no desire for life. Darkness had completely closed around her following the death of her beloved Keith. However, her wise and caring Vicar didn't give up on her. He assured her that she still had something to give and suggested when she was ready she should consider joining the bereavement team, people within the Parish who visit the recently bereaved, to sit with them, to be a listening ear and to offer compassionate friendship. It proved to be Fay's salvation, bringing healing to her own heart when she became an instrument of healing to others. She came to realise it was a God-given opportunity, one which lifted her out of her own despair and made her a means of hope and help to others.

She told me about one occasion when her near neighbour lost her husband. She didn't know the lady personally so she decided just to put a bereavement card through the door. As she stood on the doorstep clutching the envelope she found she was unable to push it through the letterbox, her heart wouldn't let her. She stood a while, eventually summoning the courage to ring the bell. When her neighbour came to the door she saw Fay and her face lit up. She threw her arms around Fay saying, "I am so glad you called, I was hoping you would. You are the only other person I know who has lost her husband. Please, come in." Fay was able to support her neighbour through the darkest days of grief and that initial contact led to a deeply nurturing friendship for them both.

Fay continued to work with bereaved people for many years. It became her calling, a God centred action, just as truly as a calling to ordained ministry – from bleak desolation to sustained redemptive action. She is now 95 years old and she speaks with great warmth about those years of privilege as she walked with those burdened by grief.

There seems to be a pattern, then, of people drawing upon their own experience of grief to reach out to others in pain. I am reminded of the words of St. Paul who wrote, 'Be steadfast, unmovable, always abounding the work of the Lord, knowing that your labour is never in vain in the Lord.'(1 Corinthians 15:58) In other words, nothing is wasted: no warm word; no loving action; no heartfelt gesture of empathy – all have value, all are life giving. Finding purpose in that way also means no sorrow is wasted. The path of pain initially perceived as a dead-end street can actually leading somewhere positive.

When Deloris and Eddie looked forward to their retirement, they had a lot to feel excited about. They had many plans for trips they hadn't managed to take while they were both working. Eddie had reduced his workload to a minimum, but one job that he was determined to finish was the refurbishment of his sister-in-law's house in London, which involved travelling to London midweek and travelling home at weekends. Eddie had never troubled Doctors much; he had always been very fit. Every week he would walk long distances in addition to his physically demanding job and also looking after his garden. He and Deloris enjoyed a healthy diet and were committed to making healthy choices. He was a man who did not make a fuss, paying no heed to coughs, colds and minor ailments. He was, however, getting some stomach pain which he dismissed as indigestion and self-medicated.

When he got off the coach one Friday his legs suddenly gave way. It was a brief episode which he told Deloris about, but dismissed as nothing. It soon became apparent, however, that he wasn't walking well, His niece in London said, "Uncle Eddie is in pain but he won't admit it." When he came home leaning on a stick, alarm bells rang for Deloris. She was an experienced nurse and made him stand without a stick. When she saw how insecure he was on his legs she was shocked and rang for an ambulance. He had concealed the problem from her and as he worked in London mid-week, she had not had the opportunity to observe him closely. Eddie talked down his symptoms to the doctors who soon wanted to send him home, but Deloris insisted on an MRI scan, she was convinced all was not well.

Within days, major surgery had been scheduled as tests had revealed a tumour on Eddie's spine. The operation was considered a success, but the cancer proved so invasive, some paralysis seemed inevitable. In the days following the operation he experienced some loss of feeling in his legs which was getting worse. Deloris was comforted by the thought that even in a wheelchair they would be together. Complications soon arose, however, in the form of blood clots which took him back into theatre, then he suffered two major heart attacks in a short space of time. The Queen Elizabeth Hospital in Birmingham was excellent. His care was superb and they kept Deloris and her family fully informed concerning all his treatment. When he was moved to the local Hospital for continued care and recuperation, unfortunately things were not so good.

Deloris was deeply unhappy about the quality of care Eddie was receiving. One day when she came in to visit, he was running a temperature and regular observations were not being recorded. When she challenged the nurse in charge, she said she would see to it then promptly went on her break. It proved to be a constant fight to get Eddie the quality of care that he deserved. Deloris fought for her Eddie. She made an appointment with the consultant to express her serious disquiet, but despite her best efforts Eddie's care never really reached a satisfactory level. Nine weeks after first being admitted, Eddie died. He never went home. Deloris came for her daily visit to discover Eddie had died shortly before her arrival. She was distressed and shocked she had not had the opportunity to say goodbye.

She sat with him in silence from 1pm to 5pm, until he was completely cold.

Deloris was dazed: unable to accept Eddie had died. She was on auto pilot, moving but feeling numb. She remembers shouting at him, "How can you be dead?" When she went to register his death, it was mentioned that she and Eddie had been the last couple to be married in that particular Congregational church. Suddenly Deloris stood and said, 'Why am I here registering his death?" and she walked out. At that point her mind refused to accept that he was gone: denial is the first chapter of the bereavement story.

In the months which followed, the worst thing for her was waking each morning. 42 years of good and loving married life make being alone a tough call. She hated waking to face another day of loneliness. Exhausted each night, she would crawl to bed having worked herself into the ground during the first year of her bereavement. She couldn't cope without having a plan for each day; if no other activity was arranged she would bake - her default position. She joined a walking group and worked hard in the garden, picking up where Eddie had left off; she went to the gym; visited her sister in London; spent valued time with her children and grandchildren; kept up all her church commitments and baked – a lot! She went to bed tired each night but still dreaded waking up next day.

Throughout the unfolding months Deloris experienced darker moments. When she tried to sort Eddie's work tools she found they spoke so eloquently of him: his skill, hard work and diligence; the means by which he had made a living for them and their children. He had been a strong, gentle man and to stand alone with his tools recalled a flood of memories. Those well-cherished tools were reminders of his character – quiet, purposeful, reliable. He had been a champion of the young people in his church and community, challenging them with questions including, "Are you making your parents proud?" After his death the young people spoke of him with warmth and appreciation, they had held him in high esteem.

Deloris decided to go back to counselling. She had been an ophthalmic nurse, trained to counsel people losing their sight, now her counselling skills were directed to grief counselling for Cruse. She brought empathy, understanding and a wealth of personal experience to the role. Out of the pain of her own sorrow she was able to bring some light to the darkness of others. Seven years on from Eddie's death, she remains deeply committed to that work. She is currently helping 4 clients regularly, in addition, delivers talks on the work of Cruse and she is an amazing fund-raiser. She always has some event in hand and organises an annual ball which is a very significant fund raiser for Cruse. Deloris has become an effective advocate for Cruse as well as a skilled and empathic practitioner. Her training and experience have helped her to understand grief and through her loss has become instrumental in helping scores of people on their own journey of healing and recovery. She honours Eddie's memory daily by the work that she undertakes. The base metal of anxiety has indeed been transmuted to the pure gold of redemptive action.

She is a strong woman in many ways. After Eddie's death she was still fretting because of the poor quality of care he had received in the local Hospital so she asked for an interview with the Hospital authorities; there she laid out her concerns and pointed out their serious shortcomings. She was given a wholly unacceptable explanation. The blame was placed at the door of agency nurses. At that point Deloris stood up and said, "Agency or not they are still nurses and you can't avoid responsibility. It is people's lives you were dealing with. You simply can't treat people like that. Things need to change." They knew they were dealing with a strong woman. She hoped that her confronting them would lead to better care for others. I also believe it was essential for her to confront the Hospital authorities as part of her own way of dealing with grief. She needed to do it for herself to ease her own pain as well as to improve things for others. That is often the case with the process of bereavement. Some things need to be revisited and dealt with so that it is possible to move on.

Her strength can also be seen in the way she has applied herself to the work of Cruse since the death of her lovely husband.

A heart which is broken is a heart which is open: open to others; open to the sorrowful and broken; open to God.

'What is life without my Love?'

It can be productive, purposeful and compassionate; a good life.

For Reflection

St. Paul writes to the Corinthian Church about the pressure and problems he and his team had experienced the province of Asia. **We were under great pressure, far beyond our ability to endure, so that we despaired even of life.** Yet there was purpose in that pain for out of it came an emphatic ability to ministry to those in similar desperate circumstances. **Praise be to the God and Father of our**

Lord Jesus Christ, the Father of compassion and the God of all comfort, who comforts us in all our troubles so that we can comfort those in any trouble with the comfort we ourselves received from God.

What have you learned through your own experience of grief that may be able to help others?

Deloris and Fay both learned how to turn that negative energy of grief into the positive energy of service. Can you identify ways in which you could act to help others who are somewhere on this journey of grief and loss?

One writer said, "There is no waste more tragic than a wasted sorrow; to endure the pain and learn nothing from it is sad indeed."

Are you ready for turning grief from the inward experience of bleak devastation to the outward expression of redemptive action?

It is no easy option. How can it be attempted?

4

LEFT BEHIND

Coming to terms with being the one who is left takes time; the sense of loss is an unwelcome daily companion. I remember saying out loud in disbelief, 'Barbara, you're dead! Why? That wasn't supposed to happen. YOU'RE DEAD!' I said it loudly - perhaps to convince myself, as my mind refused to accept it. It was an aching void in my life, now my Barbs was dead, that I could not fill. Disbelief is the first stage of grief according to Elizabeth Kubla-Ross. I think the narrative to which we had subscribed was that I would be first to go. I've no idea why, there was no logic to it; it suited my vision of life's ending. I believed Barbs would be better equipped to manage without me, then I would be to manage without her. As we approached retirement she familiarised herself with all that needed to be done by her in the event of my death.

There is only one positive aspect to her dying before me; she has been spared to pain of losing me. I don't think I am unusual in holding an ongoing conversation with my dead wife. One of the comments I have frequently made to her is, "Well Barbs, I am glad you didn't have to experience this – its hell! At least you haven't had to come to terms with a huge gap in your life where I used to be." It is a comfort to know that she was spared that heartache. It may not be much but it has helped me in the process of acceptance. Others to whom I have spoken about this confess to a similar feeling.

Tony Campolo told this story in a sermon. He had two colleagues who were brothers; both gifted theologians. Their elderly father lived on a Farm with his wife, in a long and happy marriage. One day his wife collapsed, unconscious; he couldn't revive her. He scooped up his bride in his strong arms and put her gently in his pickup truck. He drove like fury to the Hospital; but it was too late and the Doctor who tended to her gave him the bleak, unwelcome news that his beloved was dead.

The funeral was a beautiful celebration of her life and the community said their goodbyes. That evening, at home with his two boys, Dad asked the question of his theologian sons, "Where is your Mother now?" They drew upon their theological expertise and knowledge of the scripture to paint a picture of what it meant to be 'absent from the body and present with the Lord.' "Take me back to her grave," demanded their Father. They drove back to where they had laid her to rest and stood together in the empty graveyard in the still evening; looking at the mound of soil and carpet of flowers that covered her body. "It's been a good day,' said Dad, "It has been a very good day, its been a good life; and it ended as I would have wanted it to – she died first." He meant that she had been spared the pain of losing him. Ultimately, a deeply loving and tender relationship is protective of the other. He was speaking words of love that meant that the aching emptiness that had enveloped his life would never visit hers. His was the pain – hers was the peace.

It is a comforting thought for those who mourn the loss of their spouse. It may not, however, be the immediate thought. I think the farmer was unusual in lighting upon that thought so early in his experience of grief. In my conversations with those who are bereaved, it seems this thought comes after railing against the injustice; after teetering on the brink of despair; after wrestling with the pain of loneliness – then it comes, like a little ray of light through the darkness. The thought is formed from distress, 'At least my love was spared this pain, at least he or she did not have to endure this heartache.' It is a thought which rescues one from self-pity and leads to a more nurturing perspective. The heart may not be healed but perhaps it is healing.

Receiving comfort from the thought that a loved one has been spared the pain of living with loss, implies a belief in unbroken continuity. Spared the pain of loss and grief for what? To sink into the jaws of oblivion? No! Rather to enter a new and marvellously transfigured dimension of existence. For 'eye has not seen nor the ear heard the things which God has prepared for those who love Him.' (1 Corinthians 2:9) So maybe people of faith can more easily tune into this perspective. When David wept over the death of the baby he fathered with Bathsheba he said, "You will not come to me, but I will go to you." (2 Samuel 12:23) With that as an overarching meta-narrative there is true comfort in the thought, 'My loved one has been spared this pain – She will not come to me but I will go to her.'

Whether you are a person of faith or not, there is some comfort in the thought of your spouse being spared the pain of loss.

The acclaimed series, *After Life* by Ricky Gervais tells the story of a man whose wife has died, his world has fallen apart. His coping strategy is about becoming Mr Angry. He asks, 'What is the point of being nice to people, what is the point of tolerance in the face of stupidity?' His tolerance threshold has become almost non-existent. Surrounded by people who care about him, he has reached a point where grief means he no longer cares about himself. His reason for living has gone: he talks about killing himself; he is oblivious to their worries. There are two people who make him rethink - the nurse who looks after his Father, who has Alzheimer's disease, and a woman who often sits by the grave of her husband, right next to his wife's grave. They fall into conversation and speak often. She is wise, thoughtful and helps him to turn a corner to realise that him being true to his best self both honours the memory of his wife, and repairs the fractured relationship with those who care most about him.

There is a poignant moment in the final episode of the first series. They fall into conversation as they sit by their loved ones' graves. He asks her, "Are you happy?"

"Yes," she replies, "I had the most wonderful life with Stan and I have all those memories. Stan had a wonderful life too. After some thought she adds, "But I'd rather live missing him than have him to live missing me. That's how much I love him. I wouldn't change anything."

She turns her attention towards him and says, "You're a good person. Don't give up on life, it would be a waste. You may not like living much but you make the world a better place." It is one of those dramas that has something worthwhile to say about the human condition. He realigns his priorities, gets a sense of the bigger picture and resolves to return to being the best version of himself that he can be. He begins by making amends with the people he has hurt most.

I think many bereaved people who have lost their soulmate come to the same conclusion as Stan's wife. I asked Deloris, whose story appears in the previous chapter, about this. She knew exactly where I was coming from and said, "It is something I have gone over in my mind, time after time. When I think of my grief I am so glad it wasn't him." She told me that her training for Cruse had involved role play which, "was simply terrible because I had to be the one that died and imagine his emotions, his feelings along with his ability to cope day-by-day without me. I am so thankful he was spared that." That's love. Role play has great psychological power and gave Deloris such a sense of Eddie's desolation without her, that it lived with her and made her forever grateful that he had been spared the hopelessness and desperation he would have experienced without her.

What is life without my love?

For some it is a deep sense of gratitude that the other was spared the pain of loss.

"I'd rather live missing him than for him to live missing me."

For Reflection

Does the term 'Left Behind' describe your experience of bereavement?

Have you developed coping strategies for the feeling of being left?

For you is there comfort in the thought that your loved one wasn't left behind; that they were spared the pain of loss?

Could you put into words any comfort that you receive from that thought?

Jesus said to his followers in John 17 ; ***I will not leave you orphans, I will come to you.*** He will fill the vacuum in our lives if we ask him. James writing in his letter says, ***Draw near to God and he will draw near to you.*** (James 4:8)

How do you 'come close' to God?

Here are some strategies which you may already be using:

1. Be still …
2. Read a few verses of your Bible slowly and thoughtfully …
3. Keep a private note book of your spiritual journey …
4. Walk and talk to God ..
5. Immerse yourself in inspiring music …

Open your eyes and heart to the wonders of God's creation

5

SIGNS OF LIFE; SIGNS OF LOVE

I have met very few people who believe death means oblivion. At the most basic level, many believe in some kind of continuity after death. Bertrand Russell wrote "There is darkness without, and when I die there will be darkness within. There is no splendour, no vastness anywhere; only triviality for a moment, and then nothing." It is a bleak vision but, in my experience, it is embraced by only a very few people.

Many funerals are conducted today by secular celebrants. When I conduct funerals at the Crematorium, it is my habit to arrive early in an endeavour to avoid traffic hold-ups which could make me late, so am often there long before the previous funeral has concluded. A sound system conveys the proceedings to the office, so it is possible to listen in to the service. I have often checked the name and religion of the celebrant and been surprised to discover that it is a secular funeral. There is often faith-based content and references to the after-life. Frequently the speaker will present verbal pictures of Mum or Dad, alive and well, waiting in restored health, peace and harmony on the other side. Of course, Humanist funerals eschew all references to religion and belief in an after-life. Their ceremonies are always avowedly atheist, however what passes for 'non-religious' funerals are often far from that. There may be little reference to biblical faith and be of the 'home spun' variety, but religion is present. There is an inclination in the human heart to believe that death is not the end. In my experience this is more than wistful longing; it often has some conviction of faith.

A 2009 survey by Theo's Think Tank reported that 53% of people believe in the afterlife, 55% believe in heaven and 70% believe in the human soul. Whilst Shakespeare was right to describe death as the undiscovered country, "from whose bourn no traveller returns." yet in many ways, speculation about life after death has never been such a subject of fascination. In recent polls in the USA belief in heaven has not only held steady but moved upwards in the past two decades. In 2011, US surveys revealed that 81% believed in heaven. That is not to imply they all hold a central orthodox Christian position. In fact, a more 'new agey' belief in the afterlife seems to be today's favoured position. It resonates with the common claim, "I am spiritual but not religious." At least it is a starting point, which may lead to an openness to a more biblically focused vision of eternity. The Christian understanding of life beyond death is based on the resurrection of Jesus Christ. Not a peripheral issue, but the lynchpin of our faith. Jesus said, "Because I live you will live also." He is the pioneer who has conquered death and opens the way for us to follow. "I go to prepare a place for you; and if I go and prepare a place for you I will come again to receive you to myself, so that where I am there you will be also." (John 14:4)

Celtic Christians believed heaven was a kind of parallel existence; not a location at the far reaches of the universe. They would say heaven and earth are just 3 feet apart. That is where the concept of the 'thin place' comes from – where eternity breaks through into time and where the gossamer thin veil is lifted. Recently preaching in Llandudno, I made reference to the inexpressible joy which can break into our lives when the Holy Spirit is present. I quoted St. Peter; "We rejoice with joy unspeakable and full of glory." (1 Peter 1:8) After the service a visitor from Surrey met me with a broad smile and an outstretched hand. He told me of the death of his Father who loved the work of Welsh composer Karl Jenkins. He had planned his own funeral which had included some music from the Armed Man Mass by Karl Jenkins, which is a Mass for Peace. The final piece of music at the funeral was the Gloria and it is joyous. As they walked out of church into the sunshine, they did so to those joyful and glorious notes. My visiting friend, Cameron, told me he realised his Father had chosen that piece of music that for them as a reminder of the depths of joy that flows from God's heart. Cameron said he was seized with the desire to laugh and he looked up and saw a vision of his Father, much younger and radiant with joy.

He discovered later that his sister had had the same experience as she left the church.

These are the deeply significant moments and reassuring experiences which make us aware that we are standing in a thin place and heaven is very close. I believe God, in his generosity, often reveals something which is a healing moment for those deeply grieving. My own Mother was very close to her Father; she loved him deeply and always spoke of him with a smile on her face. She found it heart-breaking to see how lung cancer reduced him to a skeleton. Pain control was quite inefficient in those days and his final months were awful to witness. After his death my Mother was unable to recover from her grief -she was haunted by the memory of her Father's emancipated body and sunken, pain-filled eyes. It was sapping her energy and breaking her heart.

One night she had a vivid dream in which she saw her Father. He was youthful and smiling. He was leaning against a pillar in a beautiful Cathedral-like building bathed in light. He could not come to her but he could see her and beaming, he raised his hand and waved. When she woke she was at peace and began to heal. She knew that all was well. My Mum knew in the depths of her soul that this was a message from heaven.

St Paul in his first chapter to the Colossians mentions Epaphras, and in verse 8 writes; "he has told us how the Holy Spirit has awakened you to love." We can go through life as if blindfolded, but when the Holy Spirit awakens us to love, we will see so much more than we ever conceived possible. When I was working as a Chaplain in Armley Prison, Leeds I was visiting all prisoners in the Segregation Unit; a chaplain's statutory duty. One prisoner said, "Chaplain, will you please assist in an escape?" He was smiling broadly as he said it so I waited for the explanation. "It's not for me," he said. "It's for that pigeon in the exercise yard." From his cell window he could see a pigeon which had got stuck in a plastic bread bag. It had been pecking at crumbs on the ground and walked right inside the bread bag to enjoy every crumb. It looked up and the sky was gone! The pigeon hadn't the sense to realise it could step out backwards and regain its freedom: it was completely stuck. It had been there for hours. I set it free, simply by lifting off the plastic bag. It looked at me, blinked then soared heavenward. The prisoner looked on from his cell window "I wish you could do the same for me Chaplain!"

How often I have thought of myself like that pigeon — obsessed with small stuff; losing the wide expansive vision and getting stuck? I sometimes need the Holy Spirit to gently lift the veil and help me to look up. Maybe you do too? If we are fully awake and tuned into the Spirit we will see so much more than we ever conceived possible; signs of life and signs of love.

On a recent trip to Sydney, I was shown around the city by some dear friends. Along with the Opera House and Bridge, I really wanted to see the beautiful gothic style Cathedral of St Mary which had been built in the 1820s. One of the reasons it was important for me to see this was because of a story I remembered from the prolific writings of F W Boreham. A Baptist Minister in Melbourne, he wrote about a shop in which he and his wife liked to browse on his day off. It was run by two women, Audrey and Dorothy, whose appreciation of beautiful things was reflected in the stock they had in their shop. There were all kinds of unique artwork; pottery, paintings, ornaments; all beautifully displayed.

They were great friends; Dorothy was married but Audrey had devoted herself to the care of her Mother. When her Mother died Audrey was inconsolable. They had always been very close and now she felt herself falling apart inside; her primary reason for living was gone. As the months went by the depth of her grief was not at all assuaged. One day Dorothy said, "Take a holiday; have a complete change and give yourself time to recover." Audrey wasn't convinced this would make any difference, but she decided to take a break in Sydney. Her friend had told her, "Sydney is a great destination because you have both the city and the sea. When you've had enough of one you can enjoy the other." After a week in Sydney she did not feel the slightest bit better; grief accompanied her every step.

One day she sat on a bench in the city park and looked up to see the towers of St Mary's Cathedral. She decided to visit and sit in its stillness. She stopped at the statue of St Teresa on the north side of the nave. It is a beautiful statue and she was struck by the warmth of the Saint's smile and her arms full of flowers. Two nuns came down the aisle and spoke to her, "We see you are drawn to the statue of our dear saint, Teresa."

'Yes" said Audrey, "but why is she carrying roses?"

"That's easy to explain," said one of the nuns, "she always carried roses to give away; whenever she saw a young novice looking sad and downcast she would hand them a rose as a sign that all was well. A gesture of reassurance; the rose given with a smile said "no need for anxiety and sorrow, for all is well."

It was a beautiful story. As Audrey knelt in prayer before leaving the Cathedral she said, "Oh God, I wish someone would give me a rose to reassure me all is well with my dear Mother." At that moment, back in Melbourne Dorothy was writing a letter to her friend; she said, "Take your time on this holiday. Take the opportunity to relax and rest. Everything is fine here. Don't hurry back, come when you are ready." It was just a little note of reassurance. She was about to put it in the envelope when she noticed how beautiful the vase of roses on the counter was. She quickly took one, pressed it and popped it into the envelope, so when Audrey opened the letter in the morning, out popped a rose in answer to her prayer. She knew it was a message from heaven that all was well with her Mother, and from that moment her healing began. She returned renewed and refreshed.

What is life without my love?

Distressing; devastating and lonely? Yes, all of those things and more. Yet in the midst of our pain there is hope, a hope that beams with immortality. If we allow the Holy Spirit to awaken us, we may well see signs of life and love that we will find reassuring and deeply comforting.

For Reflection

Ephaphras said the Colossian Christians were **awakened to love by the Holy Spirit.** In our grief we often need a new awakening. We need to lift our vision for the narrow horizon of our pain to the infinite tenderness of God's love.

Are you awakened to that reality?

Are there signs of life and signs of love that come within the scope of your vision?

How can we keep our focus on life and love when death has robbed us of so much that is so precious?

Read Hebrews 12:2 **looking unto Jesus ...** the thought is to **fix your eyes upon Jesus the pioneer and perfecter of our faith.**

Is this even possible when you are on this journey of grief?

Since an awakening involves an increased awareness isn't this something we all need to pray for – increased awareness of God's loving and healing presence in our lives and and through our lives to others.

Let's pray for that and keep praying.

6

RELEASE, RELIEF, REGRET

I think it is quite a common experience to speak of a loved one's release from this life. When life has narrowed down to a prison-house of pain, departure comes to feel like a blessed release. At the point of death when laboured breathing ceases, there is a moment of leaving; the spirit has gone; release has come. It is often a moment of palpable stillness. I was with my wife when she died, sleeping in her room in the Hospice. Her breathing had become laboured; rattling and very painful to hear. Suddenly, around 2.30am, it was over. Breathing stopped. The stillness was all pervading. My children and I stood around her bed and I said a prayer of thankfulness for the vibrant life of a wonderful wife and Mother whom we loved. We hugged one another and wept. At that moment there was a sense of relief, after 18 months of her desperate battle with brain cancer, it felt like her release into life – a departure on a new journey and we were waving her off.

When St. Paul wrote to Timothy, he did so from a Roman dungeon. He knew the moment of his execution was close and he wrote, "I am being poured out like a drink offering, and the time of my departure is near." (2 Timothy 4:6) A drink offering accompanied a sacrifice and was poured out near the altar signifying the end of the sacrifice. The metaphor is employed to indicate that Paul's life is about to come to an end. The Greek word for 'departing' refers to a ship that is untied and about to set sail. It is the same word that Paul uses in Philippians 1:23 when he writes, "I have a strong desire to depart to be with Christ which is far better." It's the beginning of a voyage. Friends stand on the quayside to wave off their loved one. Release has come; a new journey has begun. Other friends wait on the quayside of destination to welcome their loved one home.

The sense of release is often accompanied by the sense of relief. I can't count the number of times I have asked, "How are you feeling," to some recently bereaved person and the response has been, "I am relieved that he/she is out of his/her suffering and is at peace." Relieved!! When you witness the death of a loved one, each new day bringing new indignity and diminishment, there is a huge level of stress. Many people are unaware of it because it creeps upon them gradually. It is a tension which quivers with negative energy. People often feel they must be strong for their loved one and their loved one feels they must be strong for them in return. They fall apart inside; balancing precariously on the edge of despair, but affecting a smile and embracing the pretence that all is well. That takes its toll in stress. At the moment of death there often comes a wave of relief; a huge sigh that says 'all the suffering is over and my love is at rest.'

A friend told me of his harrowing experience, seeing his

beloved wife wasting, suffering and losing her grip on life. He said 'it was such a relief to see her at rest; her battle was over and peace had come.' But this was short-lived. Grief, guilt and regret soon overwhelmed him. I will never forget that moment when my children and I gathered around Barbara's bed in the Hospice so soon after her death. It was a precious and peaceful moment but it was only a moment. Soon painful thoughts of regret crowded into my mind.

I discovered my regrets were often merely a desire to revisit our history. For example, I regretted that after Barbara's first stay in the Hospice I had been unable to have her back home to care for her. I had been diagnosed with my own cancer and was going into Hospital for surgery. I was also told that follow up treatment would probably be necessary for me, by way of chemo and radiotherapy. I felt I had no choice but to allow Barbara to be moved to a nursing home. We chose one with a good reputation and she was transported in the Hospice vehicle. We explained to her exactly what was happening and why, but Barbara's cognitive skills had been seriously compromised by her brain cancer. I went ahead to prepare her room by putting up photographs of the family and decorating the room with some of her favourite ornaments. Then I was called out to the vehicle to persuade Barbara to come inside.

I can still feel a lump in my throat today when I recall what was happening. She was adamantly refusing to get out of the vehicle despite all the efforts of the nurse who had travelled with her, doing her level best to encourage Barbs to go into the building. "I'm not going in there," said Barbara, adamantly. The brain cancer had robbed her of so much, but she still had her old determination and strength of character. It was a standoff. She was no more inclined to listen to my pleading than that of the nurse. Eventually she said, voice breaking, eyes filled with pain, "I thought I was going home."

Even now I can't write those words without tears and can't remember that moment without a dull weight of regret in my gut. It's a truly visceral feeling and despite 4 years since Barbara's death, its rawness is still very near the surface. "I thought I was going home."

She would never go home again.

Regrets are often more of a feeling of longing that things could have been different. Of course there will be things said or done in the turmoil of a terminal illness which will prove a focus for regret. Ordinary things are made extraordinary by the conspiracy of circumstance. Mundane things become momentous in the face of approaching death. Yet we must not lose sight of the bigger picture, regrets are both unproductive and, in the end,, quite pointless. God is with us; grace sustains us and the Holy Spirit prompts us to lift our eyes to the horizon. C.S.Lewis wrote, 'Has this world been so kind to you that you should leave with regret? There are better things ahead than any we leave behind."

On the journey of grief there are some places to be revisited and some things to avoid. For those who lost their loved one after a life-sapping illness to revisit that moment of release can be helpful.

Remember how you felt in the depth of your deep heart when the battle was over and a new journey had begun for your love. Remember that sense of relief when suffering was at an end and peace had come. But dwelling on the heartbreak of loneliness; the desperation of denial; the tidal waves of anger – all these can short circuit the process of recovery and leave you struggling. Face your sorrow but don't feed it.

Isaiah writes, "You will keep in perfect peace those whose mind is stayed on you because they trust in you." The literal meaning is "perfect peace is given to those whose minds stop at God." Stopping your mind from leaping into distressing memories and negative thoughts is never easy. We don't necessarily choose memories; they spring unbidden into our minds. Yet there is an achievable discipline of focusing our minds upon God in all His loving mercy and tenderness, bringing our wayward thoughts into captivity, letting the beauty of the Lord fill our vision.

St Paul writes in Philippians 4:8, "Finally brothers and sisters, whatever is true, whatever is noble, whatever is right, whatever is pure, whatever is lovely, whatever is admirable – if anything is excellent or praiseworthy – think about such things." Paul was encouraging people to make a conscious choice in the discipline of the mind – to focus upon the lovely, admirable, praiseworthy. Our thoughts don't need to be random and scattered, they can be focused and uplifting. We have a choice.

Travelling up the M1 from Buckinghamshire to Sheffield, which I do frequently at present, gives me the opportunity for uninterrupted thinking time. Recently as I drove, two random memories popped into my head. The first was of my wife, Barbara, looking worried and tearful when we realised the grim effects of brain cancer were already beginning to take it's toll. I put my arms round her and asked what was troubling her. She said with tears, "I'm worried about how Sarah, Paul, Katie and the boys will cope as I lose my intelligence." It was a disturbing, heart-breaking memory and very unwelcome. Four years after Barbara's death it still has the power to make me weep.

Almost immediately a second memory intruded. My daughter, Sarah, was a Press Officer for ITV, working in the Television Studios in Leeds. Because of her work she was on friendly terms with many people who are household names to the rest of us. One evening Barbs and I were relaxing in front of the TV when the phone rang. It was Sarah and she said, 'Put Mum on, Dad.' I was used to that and often tried to catch a minute or two of conversation before handing over, but tonight there was an urgent tone in her voice. Sarah said to Barbara, "Willy Russell wants to talk to you, Mum." Barbara had long admired the work of Willy Russell from Educating Rita to Shirley Valentine. She had loved teaching "Our Day Out" which was on the English National Curriculum. She couldn't believe she was talking to him. The mid-evening sleepy feeling was instantly gone. She was on her feet walking about the room in animated conversation. She asked him endless questions; she was always good at questions; chuckling and laughing as if she was talking to an old friend which, in a way, she was. It was a joy to see her so alive and intellectually vigorous. When the conversation was over she basked in the glow of it for the rest of the evening. That was a great memory which still makes me smile broadly. It had been a wonderful surprise for her. Consciously I chose that memory; lingered upon it; remembered her laughter; recalled her joy and her liveliness. That memory enriched my motorway journey.

"Whatever is lovely; admirable; excellent think about these things" (Philippians 4:8) Let your mind dwell on those beautiful, soul-stirring memories and there are lots of them.

I chose the heart-lifting; heart-warming memory and it changed my mood and filled my heart with joy and gratitude.

What is life without my love?

A whole host of emotions and release, relief and regret come into play. We need the spiritual discipline of focusing our mind upon God, and our thoughts upon memories which enrich rather than undermine. The dead-end street of regret should not be our direction of travel!

For Reflection

Pauls advice to the Philippians is good… ***Whatever is true… noble… right… pure… lovely… admirable or praiseworthy – think about such things.*** But how easy is that?

People living with loss often have the experience of being ambushed by grief – you want to focus on the peaceful and pleasant but all unbidden your mind goes to the place of maximum pain. Do you sometimes have that experience? Is it a daily occurrence at this stage in your grief journey or are you finding strategies to take your thoughts to the good place?

Is discipline of mind involved in redirecting your thoughts?

How can that be developed?

Lovely and admirable are the crowning qualities that Paul lists in Philippians 4 : 8 This is the only place in the New Testament where this word 'lovely' occurs and it means, 'that which is very dear and very precious.'

Are there memories that you could list that are 'very dear and very precious.'?

Why not take some time to write them down?

They could be a reference point to redirect your thoughts when bleak and painful memories come to besiege your mind.

Revisit Jeremiah 29:10 Read it and receive it as God's message for you.

7

PLANNING NOT DRIFTING

Finding purpose following the death of a spouse is rarely easy. If your life's purpose was fully shared, it can feel as if half of you is missing and, like a boat with one oar, you are going around in circles. My wife and I had completed our detailed plans for retirement when she was taken ill: we didn't get chance to implement those plans. Pursuing them alone seemed a bleak prospect and anyway, they had been 'our' plans not 'my' plans. One of things we had become excited about was the prospect of walking national trails; the first was to be the Cleveland Way. We had looked at the route, worked out daily distances, envisaged the 110 miles from Helmsley to Filey Brigg — over the striking North Yorkshire Moors and along the glorious Heritage Coast. Barbara was a strong walker, and we regularly undertook weekly walks in the Peak District, so whilst the National Trail was challenging, it really wasn't too daunting a challenge. The day we planned it she was full of youthful excitement and joyous enthusiasm. It was to be our first break after my retirement, but by that time her life-sapping disease had trampled our plans into the dust.

After Barbara died I couldn't walk it alone; without her every step would have been heart breaking. I needed other plans: simple steps. Daily I planned something to take me out of the house, to be inactive seemed to exacerbate the grief and loneliness. I would set myself a task; maybe something quite trivial, but it meant being out. I also tried to be around people whenever possible. I have never been a great 'joiner', apart from the church, but I made myself join a bereavement group; a Church Home Group; a Choir and I showed up to most of the live folk music gigs at my local Café. To be honest, sometimes I had to give myself a strong talking to and to push myself when I felt like collapsing in self-pity. The little plans helped. I had something to get up for every day. These little plans eventually led to bigger ones – like a trip to the Holy Land and a visit to Australia.

Learning to accept the reality of being alone and being comfortable with your own company is far from easy. When your whole life has been invested in one another in a heart-linking relationship of love, to suddenly find you are now living life alone can give rise to panic. 'Solitude is the mother country of the strong' is a statement of truth. Since solitude was not a path of your choosing you may feel you will never have the strength to cope with it; but strength can grow.

David Watson told a story about a captain of industry who had a super-efficient secretary. He came to rely on her more and more, including her skill at writing speeches. His speech-making ability improved to such a degree he was invited to more and more prestigious events as the keynote speaker. His secretary became dissatisfied she was never given credit for the speeches which were all her work. One day he rushed into the office in a hurry to get to an event where he was to address an august company of business people. "Is this my speech?" His secretary confirmed that the large envelope on his desk was indeed 'his speech.' He dashed off without so much as a 'thank you.'

He had no time to look through the speech but he was confident. After being introduced, he stood up and worked his way through the first page of the speech, going well and gaining momentum. The first page concluded with the words, "So now I want to consider this subject under the following six headings." He turned the page to find it completely blank, except for the following sentence in large letters, "You're on your own now.."

David Watson used the story to illustrate how the disciples may have felt when Jesus had been taken from them. They can be pretty bleak and accurate words for the person who has had their spouse taken from them by death. 'You're on your own now." Yet finding the strength to be alone is both important and possible.

David Watson went on to speak of the coming of the Holy Spirit into the lives of the disciple making good the promise of Jesus, not to leave them orphaned. He spoke of the transformative power of the Holy Spirit who brought courage and conviction to the Apostles so they were able to 'eat their food with gladness' and pursue God's mission with boldness. Finding the presence of the Holy Spirit in our own lives serves to alleviate a sense of aloneness and enables us, however tentatively, to formulate plans which tap into a bigger purpose.

Embracing stillness can be a deeply healing experience.

The Psalmist writes, "Be still and know that I am God." (Psalm 46:10) We can engage with the enriching experience of the Spirit in the depths of our hearts when we choose stillness.

It is there moments of solitude can feed the soul. I, like many others like noise and my radio is tuned permanently to BBC Radio 4. There is a range of excellent and thought-provoking programmes, but quite honestly it is often just the sound of the human voice makes me feel less alone. For others it is music and for others, podcasts direct through earphones. It took a degree of self-discipline to switch off and embrace the silence; to relax into it; to breath, to trust, to rest in God. First comes stillness and then, knowledge. While you are wrapped in stillness and remain, not rushing away, you can step into knowledge. A new and heart-warming conviction grows "...I AM GOD." It is a knowledge beyond all shadow of doubt or illusion that the God who is love affirms you; holds you; sets you free from drift and lifts your vision to purpose. In the stillness you know it.

'Be still and know that I am God.'

I am not entirely opposed to drifting when drifting forms part of the plan; there are occasions when drifting through a day is recuperative; when you switch off from everything, and just take time to 'be' without succumbing to the pressure to 'do.' Drifting is a driving technique for racing drivers, which occurs when a driver deliberately oversteers so traction is lost in the rear wheels but control is maintained driving decisively through a corner. Here is drift which has purpose and does not involve any loss of control. Drifting as a recovery technique has value, but drifting as a way of relinquishing control can be disastrous.

WHAT IS LIFE WITHOUT MY LOVE?

In November 2018 I fulfilled a long-held ambition to travel to Australia, reconnecting with old friends on their home territory whilst experiencing the adventure of Australia. I recently found a note on my IPad which I had made on the last leg of the journey from Dubai to Perth. I had written;

"There is nothing like a 10-hour flight to set the mind drifting. It is liminal time – a time between.

I remember when Barbs and I were moving from Firvale to Aston, I was leaving a parish I loved and was moving to be Team Rector of Parishes that I, as yet, did not know. It was only a few miles and yet, in some ways, it was a big journey. Our furniture was packed, loaded and we were staying in a hotel overnight. We had left our home and not yet arrived at our new one. What a strangely atmospheric yet wonderful evening we had – deeply reflective and full of wonder at life's mystery. We talked about our children; our hopes and aspirations; yet somehow we were 'in the moment.' Now here I was in mid-flight; a time between, full of memory and reflection. I didn't expect it be emotional. Yet here are tears, unbidden and unexpected, lubricating my memories.

So here I am – alone, liminal time. Life is good – despite loss. Barbs was so ready to embrace life; I loved her for that. Her enduring love helps me to embrace life too. She was always two steps ahead of me and I feel she is still – but she beckons me on. I'm learning."

If you feel yourself drifting, go with it. Let the current carry you. Learn from it. Relax into it. Let go of stress. 'Let go and let God,' is not just a neat aphorism it is also a really apposite statement of truth. Let go of anxiety and panic, you are safe in the ocean of God's love. This is a completely safe environment for drifting because you cannot drift into danger. Isaiah writes; "In returning and in resting you will be saved; in quietness and confidence with be your strength."(Isaiah 30:15)

Returning from turmoil and heartbreak to the God whose tender care is beyond all human computation, then resting in Him, brings quietness and confidence leading to renewed strength. That is a secure place from which to formulate further plans.

Many years ago I was invited to be the preacher at a church anniversary weekend. The church elder who contacted me was quite verbose. He rang a few days before the date I was due to be there and said, "Brother, I am ringing to enquire about your projected dispositions." I found it amusingly cumbersome but it became one of those private joke phrases between my wife and myself, "Shall we discuss our projected dispositions?" we would sometimes say to one another. It was one of the things I asked myself frequently after Barbara died. Over my Monday morning Weetabix I would say to myself 'now what are my projected dispositions for this week.' Though plans don't have to be slavishly followed, having immediate; medium term and long-term plans help build perspective and purpose.

For me the medium and longer term plans included things that I could not have done with Barbara. For my 70th birthday I bought myself a trip to the Holy Land; something that we could not have planned to do together. I talked about the possibility once or twice but couldn't persuade her. Guided tours of holy sites were not her idea of a holiday - even the closest of couples don't have complete unanimity about everything! There may well be things that you could not do together because you didn't fully share the same interests, but now you are free to fulfil those plans and there may be a new sense of freedom in that. Welcome it. It is not an act of disloyalty; it is saying 'yes' to life.

Then there is the bigger plan; God's plan. If you are living with bereavement it is sometimes hard to shake the thought there is no 'big plan' and that life is just a series of random events. The concept of the 'big plan' can feel like a bad joke in poor taste when all your careful plans have crumbled into dust. It may be hard to find purpose. Yet as we still the turbulence of our hearts and invite God to calm our anxious thoughts, He will prompt us to an awareness that we are still part of His greater plan. 'Whether you turn to the left or to the right you will hear a voice behind you saying, "This is the way, walk in it."' Isaiah 30:21

Even through the processes of grief, we can live God-guided lives. The words of Jeremiah 29:10 are for us too; "I have plans for you - to prosper you, not to harm you - but to give you hope and a future."

What is life without my love?

It can become a life with renewed purpose; a life in which the plan of God unfolds.

For Reflection

Do you think that drifting has any merit in your experience?

How can it be a positive experience?

Does the saying, 'Let Go and Let God.' Have any

meaning for you?

What does it really mean?

Can you choose stillness?
How do you benefit from that choice?

Liminal time is often a time to refocus – the time between and perhaps the time to embrace the bigger plan. How do you see your own future?

Revisit Jeremiah 29:10
I have plans for you – to prosper you, not to harm you – but to give you hope and a future.
Read it slowly and prayerfully and receive it as God's message for you.

8

ANNIVERSARIES AND SPECIAL DATES

When I was a Prison Chaplain it didn't take me long to realise that Christmas was a very difficult time for the prisoners. Some tried to take the view that it was just another day but it really wasn't. As Christmas was approaching I would go around the wings with invitations to our Christmas services in the Chapel. D wing was renowned for being the place for hardened criminal types. As I went around the landings one prisoner addressed me with a degree of aggression, "I would stop handing those out if I was you; Christmas has been cancelled on D Wing."

"I know Christmas is tough when you're banged up," I said, "I get that but I just want everyone to have an opportunity to get hold of the real meaning of Christmas, and you can experience that even in prison."

"And I'm telling you that nasty accidents can happen on D Wing." He said, "For example it would be sad if a Chaplain was to fall down the metal stairs from the top landing to the bottom just before Christmas. That could happen," he looked at me menacingly.

I continued to distribute the invitations - but took care to keep looking over my shoulder!

At that time, we had a 'Lifer' called Ben (not his real name) in the prison, who had come to faith 10 years into his sentence, in a-life changing encounter with Christ. He had by now served 24 years. He had trained as a Methodist local preacher during his years inside and when he took the exams, he was permitted to go out on day release to preach in the local Methodist Church. It was quite an achievement for him to become a certificated local preacher. I was glad to give him an opportunity to preach in the prison chapel from time to time, and had invited him to deliver the Christmas Day sermon that year. There were about 60 men in chapel that Christmas morning; he pulled no punches,

"Many of you will be crying at some point today, alone in your cell. You'll be thinking of friends and family celebrating without you. You put on a brave face because that what we do in here. We've got to present a hard image but the reality is that we're falling apart inside. I know - I have been where you are. This is my 24th Christmas inside and I wouldn't have survived if I hadn't discovered the true meaning of Christmas."

He went on to talk about the babe of Bethlehem; born in Bethlehem, 'The House of Bread,' who is the Bread of Life and who alone can satisfy the deep hunger of the human heart. I watched the men sinking into their seats as he spoke of their desolation and then straighten up when he spoke of hope and new life.

Christmas is really just the 25th of December, another day in the calendar, but it is invested with such poignancy when it is also linked with loss.

Christmas is tough for the bereaved: so many painful and vivid memories come flooding back. My wife had a colleague and close friend, Pam, (not her real name) whose husband died suddenly. They had no children and had always spent Christmas in a hotel by the sea in North Yorkshire. It was a beautiful, peaceful setting and they loved the location and celebrating Christmas together there. Derek (not his real name) had died in the September and Pam decided to go to the North Yorkshire hotel for Christmas once again. I think she thought it would be a way of coming to terms with her grief, but instead it was heart-breaking and utterly desolating. She cut the trip short and drove home. On those occasions of celebration, you can be very vulnerable and may need safe and supportive people around.

In my family we have introduced a new Christmas tradition which includes Barbara. Our whole family clusters together for a photograph. We have full glasses ready for a toast and at the heart of the cluster is a big photograph of Barbara. Maybe someone will share a joyous memory which prompts laughter. We raise our glasses and drink a toast to her memory. She is still at the centre and the symbolism is important. She is deeply loved, remembered and always included in our Christmas celebrations. We take a photograph to mark the occasion. Barbara died before our little grandson, George, was born and never met her, but I love the fact that he is growing up with her as part of his Christmas. The Christmas before his second birthday he held the picture, kissed it and said, "Granny Barbs,' and laughed. Barbs would have loved that. He will always know about Granny Barbs. I have spoken with other families who have adopted a similar new tradition to include their loved one in Christmas in a way which is meaningful and celebratory.

Remembrance is the last gift of love. When I was Vicar of St Cuthbert's in Sheffield, I was drawn to a beautiful stained-glass window commemorating the death of a young chorister- Hugh Kelsey - who had been killed in the Great War. The window was strikingly beautiful and depicted him in his choir robes, and, standing beside him, was Jesus – loving and welcoming. I thought of the heart-broken parents who had paid for this beautiful window to be installed. When it came to Remembrance Sunday I referenced him in my sermon. I imagined his voice blending with the others, filling the sacred space of the parish church with the high praises of God. Perhaps he sang the opening verse of 'Once in Royal David's City' at Midnight Mass.

I found an old photo in a little used metal cupboard in the choir vestry, and there he was in football kit, sitting in the front centre row clutching the ball. I imagine the photo indicates he played centre forward in the church football team and was, perhaps, 14 or 15. I imagined him dribbling past opponents to score a winning goal to the acclaim of his fellow team mates. Perhaps he cherished an ambition to play for Sheffield Wednesday or Sheffield United; there was no way of knowing where his allegiances lay, but in keeping with almost every Sheffield boy who could kick a ball he would have had his dreams.

I painted a word picture of him and imagined that fateful morning when the news of his death had come through. I wondered if the Vicar had announced the sad news and if his parents had been in that service amongst friends who loved them and shared their loss. Hugh came to embody our memories and was a true focus for our grateful remembrance of all those who gave their lives to secure peace and safety for our world. The point, clearly made, was that he had been a real person with hopes, dreams and aspirations; surrounded by people he loved and who loved him. Every Remembrance Sunday while we remember our national loss in moments of silence, we stand rapt in thought. Pain and pride mingle: here is hurt and heartbreak, but hope and healing remain.

Maybe that is always the way with the flood of memory which comes on anniversaries and special days; there is hurt but healing too; pain mingles with pride; heartache indeed, but tempered by hope.

Anticipating significant dates is a bit like seeing a dark storm gathering on the horizon. It is on your horizon and there is no way of avoiding it; your path may have been lit with welcome light, but grey skies lie ahead. That is the experience of many.

A friend described how bleak October has become for her; many memories spring unbidden to her mind including the sudden downturn of her husband's condition; treatment that brought discomfort but no healing; vivid memories of hospitalisation and desperation; fighting to live; fighting for breath and losing the fight. Her memories seem to line up like paratroopers ready to drop into her consciousness throughout the month. She dreads these October blues. We all have stormy horizons to face, yet gently unfolding rhythms of grace can help us to face those storms. An upward look of trustful silence; a place of prayerful stillness; the warm affirmation of God's love; all help us to come through the storm to sunshine once again.

Lynnette's husband Dave died at 57. He suffered from early onset Lewy Dementia disease so his final years were hugely distressing, Lynette spoke of Dave's illness as 'the long kiss goodbye.' He had been an outstanding sportsman and a skilled musician; remembered by many with great affection. A golfing award was established in his memory and competitors who win the contest are proud to hold up the trophy and remember with deep respect the man whose name it honours.

I asked Lynnette how she deals with anniversaries. She said on his birthday they have a cake and the grandchildren sing happy birthday to Grandpa in heaven. They love that, even though they never met him. Celebrating his birthday together has become an important part of family activity. In this way Lynnette keeps his memory alive, and passes on to the next generation a deep appreciation of the person he was and the legacy he has left behind. Lynnette told me that she and Dave had a great marriage.

"I am grateful for every day that Dave and I spent together." She added, "I feel most nostalgic on our wedding anniversary. Others can share in birthday and Christmas celebrations, but the memories of our wedding day are deeply personal: our day. Dave was a true worshipper and a great musician and, on our anniversary, I put on worshipful music and listen; remembering how it inspired us both. It lifts my spirit Godward and makes me feel closer to Dave. He was in my past; he may not share my present, but he will be in my future." It has been nine years since David died, and although Lynette says it doesn't get easier, she also observes, "With God's help I have learned to deal with it."

That is really the key: God's help. G.A. Studdert Kennedy

was the most famous Chaplain of the Great War, becoming known an Woodbine Willy because of his habit of handing out cigarettes and Bibles to troops in the trenches. He wrote a volume of poetry called 'Unutterable Beauty', which included a lot of war poetry. One poem, 'A Mother Understands', pictures a Mother kneeling at the Communion rail. She has received the devastating news that her son has been killed and the poem conveys her thoughts as she kneels with hands outstretched, to receive the bread and wine:

Dear Lord, I hold my hand to take
Thy Body, broken here for me,
Accept the sacrifice I make,
My body, broken, there, for Thee.

His was my body, born of me,
Born of my bitter travail pain,
And it lies broken on the field,
Swept by the wind and rain.

Surely a Mother understands
Thy thorn-crowned head,
The mystery of Thy pierced hands
—the Broken Bread.

Christian faith has a cross at its heart; the incarnation means that God in Christ enters fully into our suffering. In fact, he suffers with us; and, of course, he suffered for us. "For we do not have a high priest who is unable to empathise with our weaknesses, but we have one who is tempted in every way, just as we are — yet without sin." (Hebrews 4:15) 'With Gods help' said Lynnette and she has proved that over her difficult years of bereavement since her beloved Dave died. 'When the way was hard, God carried me,' she said.

Our reality is that Jesus is not a remote high priest, austere and distant but instead is a constant companion who has the capacity to empathise and encourage; to sympathise and to save.

Penelope Wilcock has written a well-researched book entitled, 'Spiritual Care of Dying and Bereaved People.' She speaks of Jesus at the Last Supper with his disciples, 'The Lord Jesus the same night he was betrayed, took bread, and broke it and gave it to his disciples saying, "This is my body …'

"People who are facing death and grief understand the symbolism of night, 'the night when he was betrayed.' They know what it means to be betrayed – to be let down by their bodies, to live in a world no longer reliable, to feel life itself turn its back on them. They know the dark night of betrayal that is encountered in helplessness; and it means a lot that, on the same night that he was betrayed Jesus took the bread into his hands and, as he tore it, offered his own brokenness as a gift, a fellowship, a grace to be shared by the helpless and broken in every generation."

What is life without my love?

It doesn't need to be a series of bleak anniversaries – each date can be transformed into a life-affirming celebration. I was moved when Lynnette claimed, "I am grateful for every day which Dave and I spent together,"

Anniversaries and special dates have become a focus of that thankfulness.

Maybe they can be for you too.

For Reflection

What is your experience of anniversaries?

Do you dread the thought of the anniversary of your loved ones death or have you found ways of redeeming it and making it a focus of healing and hope?

The writer to the Hebrews gives us a picture of Jesus, not as a distant high priest figure who is remote and unable to empathise with us in our pain. On the contrary he was **tested in every way – just as we are - yet he was without sin.** He is a sympathising Saviour who has a deep capacity of empathy.

Does that vision of the Living Lord help as anniversaries loom on your horizon?

Have you got family traditions about anniversaries that are creative and and purposeful?

Are there ways in which you could develop a new way of celebrating the life that you and your love shared together and rejoicing in the gift that God gave you in one another?

9

CHILDREN:
THE GIFT THAT KEEPS ON GIVING

There is such a deep sorrow at the loss of a parent; when the relationship has been rich and loving it is a devastating loss. Adults feel like small children again when a beloved parent dies. Memory reaches back to joyous moments of childhood when the parent and child bond was deeply nurturing. There is often an acute sense of being orphaned. Scott was a loving son to both of his parents whom he lived with in the family home. They were my neighbours and I thought 'how lovely to have an adult son still living with his parents in a loving family unit.' However, his Mum died of brain cancer and his Dad, who had suffered a serious stroke a few years earlier, needed Scott more than ever. They drew closer together finding comfort in the pain of mutual loss. Quite suddenly Scotts's Dad died also. Shortly after his Dad's death Scott posted on Facebook, "I'm an orphan please somebody adopt me." That reflects his humour but also the ache in his heart. He was forty-two but feeling orphaned.

It has been almost 3 and a half years since my wife Barbara died and, last week, sitting having a coffee with my daughter Sarah I asked, "What do you miss most about Mum?" Almost immediately silent tears ran down her cheeks. Sarah is a very strong person -even as a child her crying was seldom loud vocal outbursts but her tears often flowed silently. I was moved by the familiar sight of those silent tears and almost regretted asking the question that caused them. "I miss talking to her Dad, telling her the things I know she would love to hear, about my day; my job; my plans." Every day they had talked or texted about a whole host of things; often quite trivial in themselves. Barbara was always hugely enthusiastic about our children's challenges and choices and was always interested in the most mundane things in their lives. She added, "I bought a new vacuum cleaner the other day and I wanted to tell Mum. She would have loved it; it's so efficient and powerful. I know it's trivial but I know Mum would have been so enthusiastic about it."

One of the activities of the Church Home Group I attended after Barbara's death, was to write a letter to ourselves. We wrote it at the year-end to be opened at the end of the following year. It was about hopes, wishes and personal aspirations. About my children I wrote, 'Be as good a Dad as you can be – Paul and Sarah have lost their Mum. Maybe I can be more caring, loving and available.' When I opened that letter, 12 months later, I felt I had been as good a Dad as I could be and had fulfilled those aspirations. I also felt they had been extraordinary children – a son and daughter to be proud of – loving, thoughtful and caring. We had drawn closer and were available to support each other in our mutual loss.

Family dynamics can change significantly when a parent dies. There may be unresolved issues which complicate things. Emotions are intense in the experience of grief, and sometimes underlying problems can emerge. If the person who has died was the glue that held the family together, there is the all too obvious danger of a family falling apart. And that is a tragedy. The whole grieving family need to keep their eye on the bigger picture and make a conscious decision to pull together and honour the memory of their loved one by being there for one another.

I love the way in which my friends, the Watt family, have dealt with their shared grief. Bill was an extraordinary human being. When he died of pancreatic cancer the whole community mourned him. none more so than his wife and their 5 sons, along with their partners and children. A plaque now adorns the wall of Hope Centre, Coventry honouring his memory. The Centre came into being as a result of his energy, compassion and determination. It is a multifaceted ministry which touches the lives of the most needy, broken and marginalised of our society. Bill was all heart and a true pastor. I watched a video of him giving a talk about Hope and its ministry. When he spoke about the broken and hurting people helped by the Hope Centre, he choked up with emotion and needed to get out his hanky to wipe tears several times. He was a visionary, an activist, he was passionate about the community and is hugely missed.

His family talk about Bill a lot and, in a very natural way, recount the things he said and did. They are a constant support to their Mother, lightening her burden and bringing her joy. They remember the funny things that happened and there is frequent laughter as well as some tears. They have a family "WhatsApp" group and there is daily communication; poignant memories as well as lively humour. They are very close and a great example of a caring family, for whom the contours of grief are encompassed in love. I mention them here because although they were devastated by Bill's death, they are an inspiration in the way they honour Bill's memory - being available to one another and pulling together.

The question arises, what about couples who are childless? To face life alone without the loving support and care of children is a really tough call. You need people around you when you are living with grief; people who care; people you can trust and with whom you feel safe. It may be extended family, it can be friends - more likely a combination of both.

After my wife died I felt a bit adrift from Church. We had just retired and moved to a new area so I didn't have my church family around me. One day, I was walking along the road when I was greeted by a young woman whom I knew from my old parish. She had moved and was living close by. She asked if I had settled into a Church yet? I said I hadn't and she extended an invitation to visit the church she was attending, which was a 'church plant' from a large and well-known church in the city. What clinched it for me was when she said, "I'm sure you would love our home group; it is warm, friendly and welcoming and there's a mixture of ages."

That group proved to be a blessing to me. It was not earnestly super-spiritual or gushingly intrusive. It seemed like extended family – supportive without being overwhelming.

There was prayer, study, laughter, food, conversation and friendship. In that church the groups were called 'Growth Groups' and so the overall focus was on spiritual growth; growing together in purpose and faith. Most successful churches have such groups, recognising the human need to belong – not just to a congregation but to a smaller family type group. There are a host of names; Care Groups; Share Groups; Life Groups; Cell Groups and Link Groups.

Lynnette and Dave ran a Link Group together and, since Dave's death, Lynnette continues to run that group as well as an over 60s group, with another widow. A number of people who have joined are themselves recently bereaved and are finding it most helpful. Lynnette says, "Small groups are great for building relationships and sharing life experiences which certainly helped me to keep going after Dave's death."

When my son, Paul, was six we were living in Birmingham. At Christmas Barbara's Mum and Dad came to stay, looking forward to the excitement of Christmas morning and seeing the children open their presents. At around 2am on Christmas morning I heard the stairs creak. "Oh no," I said to Barbara, "that sounds like Paul on the stairs." I got up quickly to send him back to bed until a more acceptable hour. I found him, however, not going down the stairs but coming back up. "Father Christmas has been Dad," he said. A bit dismayed I said, "You haven't opened your presents have you, Paul?" He looked a bit surprised, "Yes, of course," he said, "I'm going back to bed now." He had had his own private Christmas, all by himself! Barbara and I wondered about re-wrapping his presents but he had ripped off the paper and it was shredded. All his joyous excitement was private that Christmas! It reminded me that joy is meant to be shared so that others can feel its warmth. Similarly, grief is not meant to be an entirely private matter, it should be shared so that others can come alongside with heartfelt empathy to shoulder a little of the burden.

When he was a young man John Wesley was very affected by reading spiritual classics such as Jeremy 'Taylor's Holy Living and Holy Dying.' He was very earnest and single minded and may have harboured a desire to make his journey God-ward a rugged, individual enterprise, but he met someone whom he called 'a serious man,' who said to him, "Sir, you wish to serve God and go to heaven. Remember you cannot serve Him alone. You must therefore either find companions or make them. The Bible knows nothing of solitary religion." Those words fastened themselves upon his consciousness and he often repeated them. They became woven into his theology and practice; The Bible knows nothing of solitary religion; so the small group was born in the life of early Methodism in the form of the Class Meeting. It is understood that this was key to the amazing success of early Methodism. It is not just a phenomenon of the church in the late 20th century and early 21st century, because Wesley also understood the deep need of the human heart for life-linking relationships. Of course, the need to belong is not just for the journey of grief, but for the journey of life.

Those who are close to their grandchildren have a gift beyond words. My wife didn't get to meet our newest grandson, George. She died in 2016 and he was born in 2018. When I asked my son what he most missed about his Mum, without hesitation he said, "In my imagination I can see how she would have been with George; she would have been overjoyed at his arrival and she would have lavished love and attention upon him. Her laughter would have filled the house." My heart always aches a little when I see his beaming smile and hear him say "Grandpa" or rather, 'Bampa!" It aches with love but it also with the poignant pain of Barbara's loss. Last Christmas we held our usual Christmas tradition as a family toasting Barbara with her photo at the centre. Afterward George took the picture, held it up and announced, "Granny Barbs," with a beaming smile. He already knows who she is, but he will never meet her.

I feel for those who do not have the comfort of grandchildren in their bereavement. I believe children should have a place in all of our lives in some way. When I was a small boy I was slightly annoyed with both of my grandfathers, simply because they were dead. They had checked out before I arrived in this world. I had two warm and loving grandmothers, but I longed for a Grandad. There was a bench on the corner at the bottom of our street and the old men would congregate there, leaning on their sticks, smoking their pipes and reminiscing. I used to go and join them. It must have looked a bit incongruous, a chubby little boy sitting among the ancients! Sadly, today it would be a worrying scenario, but I had four or five surrogate grandads who welcomed me to their company. I remember one conversation between two of them. One said, "You fought in the last war didn't you Albert?"

"I fought in both," he said. "I was just old enough to serve in the first one and just young enough to serve in the second one." I remember thinking how exciting it must have been to fight in two wars! But there was a tone in his voice which suggested otherwise. I listened in to their conversation and looked up to them. My favourite was Mr Parsons who made me a sturdy little spade with my own name engraved on it. My Dad allocated a tiny bit of his garden to me where I put that spade to good use.

Children are not the exclusive possession of parents, but in one sense they belong to us all. We all have a responsibility to care for the children of our world. It is true to say that within the family of the church we can find enriching connections. Safeguarding is there to afford protection to our children within Church life, but we are essentially a family, the old need the young and the young need the old. Even those who don't have their own children can find great joy in children of the church family and find comfort and inspiration in them.

What is life without my love?

It must include children - loving and life affirming, reminding us that there is a future for the human family.

For Reflection

One of the much-repeated issues during the Corona Virus crisis has been the longing to hug children and grandchildren. The lock down was almost unbearable for many. It so highlighted the need for touch. It made us aware of the healing in a hug.

How would you put into words the value of the gift of children and grandchildren?

Isaiah 40:11 ***God tends his flock like a shepherd; he will gather the lambs in his arms; he will carry them in his bosom.***

Isaiah gives us a beautiful picture of how God holds us, his children, with such loving tenderness.

Is Gods loving care of you, his child, reflected in your loving care of your children/grandchildren?

Is it conceivable that just as we take joy and delight in our loving relationship with our natural family that God also takes delight in us as his loving family?

The Presiding Bishop of the American Episcopal Church, Very Revd Michael Curry said, "If it isn't about love it isn't about God."

There is much pain in family relationships where loves seems to have died. How can we nurture the love in our family so that it reflects God's love?

10

THE PLACE OF PILGRIMAGE

My Mother died in Sleaford when I was 26; I was married to Barbara and living in South Wales at that time. It was 2 days before Christmas, a Sunday and the Carol service was that evening. I had been keeping vigil by my Mother's bed but had travelled back to South Wales to conduct those Christmas Services in my church. My Dad rang at 3pm to break the news. I walked out into the garden and looked up at the leaden skies. She had suffered 18 harrowing months of bowel cancer. I thought about all that she had endured and I was angry with God. I said out loud, "Heaven had better be something really spectacular to make up for all that pain and suffering." I continued to look skyward half expecting an answer. The answer came, as it so often does, in a quiet sense of inward reassurance. I went to Church, preached my Carol Service sermon and then drove to Lincolnshire.

After the funeral in Sleaford, my sister and I paid for a

simple monument for the head of Mum's grave bearing her name, 'Linda Jennings 1918 – 1973'. We had established an earthly spot to visit and lay flowers; a peaceful corner of a graveyard in which to be still and wrapped in memory. Only a few short years later, however, our entire family had moved many miles away and no one was left to visit regularly. That wouldn't have troubled my Mum, who always believed that memories in the heart are more important than monuments of stone, yet there are times when I need to drive to that little Lincolnshire town and visit my Mums grave. It has the feel of a pilgrimage about it.

She died before our children arrived and on one visit I wrote her a letter about the children. I told her what wonderful human beings they are and how she would have loved them. I wrote about their achievements, their outstanding characters and how Barbs and I were so proud of them. I wrapped the letter in flowers and laid it on her grave. At that point many years had intervened since her death, but for me it was a profound moment of symbolic communication with my beloved Mum.

Is it important to have a place of memory to visit; a physical spot that is redolent of precious reminiscence? I think for many people it is. It may not be a grave. For some, it is a seat looking out at a view that was special to the deceased. For my friends, the Watt family, it is a mountain in Wales where they go every Easter for a family holiday, with as many as 20 family members gathered together. They built a cairn at the top of a mountain some years ago, and they walk up the mountain every year to place something new among the stones of the cairn. There are lots of family memories there in that special place where some of Bills ashes rest in a little casket. The grandchildren have placed rainbow painted stones and little notes to Pappy. It is a special place in the palpable peace and stillness of the mountains. No one has ever disturbed it and it is so remote that few people will pass it. It is their place of family pilgrimage which has become an integral part of a fun-filled family holiday. Memory and joy often go hand-in-hand; tinged with sorrow, of course, but their Easter family time in Wales rings with the celebration of the life of a wonderful man.

After the death of my wife I found retirement held no delights for me, I needed to engage my heart and mind in Christian Ministry again. The opportunity I looked and prayed for came in the shape of a non-stipendiary role as part-time associate minister at St Mary's, Denham. It is a joy to be part of an energetic team led by the Rector, Christoph, who is a very gifted and highly motivated leader. The village is beautiful and the 12th century church is a gem. I was interested to make the discovery that Denham had been the much loved home of Sir John Mills. His home, bearing a blue plaque is right next to the church. His association with the church was strong. I am told that he was a regular attender at church and on the reading rota. I imagined popping into the Parish Church and discovering that the lesson was being read by an internationally acclaimed star of stage and screen! Yet of course in St Mary's he was just another reader; humble and happy to read God's word in his church.

He is buried in the churchyard and, in fact, his grave is located just over the fence from the bottom of his garden. He was born in 22nd February 1908. I noticed that there was a single white lily placed lovingly on his grave on February 22nd and also another placed on the seat in the churchyard facing directly towards the church. It is a beautiful place to sit and contemplate the splendour of the ancient church. The seat was given by Sir John and Lady Mills to celebrate his 90th birthday. On his birthday someone remembered him with gratitude; who knows whether family, fan or friend, but the understated gesture of the single flower speaks of loving memory. To have a spot on this earth where affectionate memory finds focus has deep and real value.

I found another famous name on a headstone in St Mary's Graveyard, that of Sir Roger Moore. I was confused by the inscription which says "Resting in Monaco." I thought it was an attempt at ironic humour until I attended the wedding of my friend's son, Joshua, who is an Anglican Priest. His Best Man was Anglican Chaplain to the expat community in Monaco and had conducted the funeral of Sir Roger saying the words of committal over his grave in Monaco. His British home was Denham, however, and his memorial has been added to the headstone of his beloved stepdaughter in St Mary's Churchyard. It was clearly of importance that there should be a place of remembrance in the United Kingdom as a focus of glad and grateful memory. The grave is flanked by two bay trees which have been planted on either side of the headstone. The bay tree figures frequently in Greek mythology; a handsome evergreen which symbolises courage and strength. I think it is true to say that Sir Roger had those qualities along with a mischievous and self-effacing sense of humour. Resting in Monaco, but remembered in Buckinghamshire. He is not there but his memory is.

Sometimes it is a matter of space rather than place. I was talking to Joan whose husband had died 20 years ago when she told me she is seriously contemplating having a request in her will to have her husband's memorial removed after her death. She regularly places flowers on it, but anticipates a time, following her own death when it will become neglected. Her only daughter lives on another continent and she doesn't want her to have the additional pressure of having responsibility for the care of her parents' grave.

She also remembers the words of her beloved Father, "I'd rather have no flowers than dead flowers." Joan's daughter will always remember her wonderful parents but won't need a marble inscription to do so. She will find her own space for grateful memory.

When I was Team Rector of Aston, I had a responsibility for the Church of the Holy Trinity in the beautiful village of Ulley. In 2014 I had the privilege of dedicating a garden of remembrance there, where cremated remains could be buried, marked by a memorial tablet. Little did I realise on that sunlit afternoon, that my Barbs would be among the first whose remains would be placed there. I added the words 'A Radiant Life" to her memorial which is a fitting description of the person she was. But I placed only half of her ashes there and kept the other half for scattering under 'our tree.' One of our regular walks was Mam Tor, and from there along the ridge to Back Tor. On the ridge there is a single pine tree. There is a copse of pine a few hundred yards down the hill, but this one stands alone in splendid isolation, proudly occupying its own space. We loved that brave tree and said to each other, 'Let's get our kids to place our ashes here when we have gone."

So the other half of Barbara's ashes are there. I love that place. I can see the tree from miles away. I look up from Castleton to see it clinging to its ridge and around it cluster hosts of precious memories and it brings me joy. Holy Trinity is the place and the Mam Tor tree is the space. I value both but I can travel to that space in mind and imagination any time. I also have a beautiful water colour of it hanging in my hall which we bought together.

I mentioned in an earlier chapter that I visited the Holy Land after my wife died. I was so looking forward to visiting the Church of the Holy Sepulchre – to see the actual place where our Lord's body was laid to rest on Good Friday and from which He arose on Easter Day. I queued to enter the little sanctuary place where His body is believed to have lain. I reverently placed my hand on the very spot and prayerfully lingered for a moment. I felt nothing: no awe filled moments of inspiration; no wondrous sense of participation – nothing!

Then I visited the Garden Tomb. How evocative is that beautiful space! Surrounded by the colour and fragrance of the garden and peering into the empty tomb you can almost hear the angel whisper, "He is not here, He is risen," and you listen for His gentle footfall on the dewy grass. It is all so redolent of resurrection. Is it authentic? Highly unlikely! General Gordon made the connection in 1883 when he saw the skull shaped hill above it and thought he had discovered Calvary. But it is regarded as 8th century by some archaeologists. I asked our Palestinian Christian guide for his thoughts on the Garden Tomb versus the Church of the Holy Sepulchre. He gestured widely with his arms and he said, "The empty tomb is in the Garden and in the Church; it is in India; Africa; Afghanistan and Iraq; England and USA; because Christ is Risen and his living presence can be encountered anywhere and everywhere." With a broad smile he opened his arms into an even wider gesture. He was right of course. A place of remembrance has undoubted value. But geographical location is not the supreme thing. A space where the heart can be ignited with beauty of precious memory can be almost anywhere.

Visiting a grave or a memorial space can seem like a bleak prospect but the thing about pilgrimage is that you carry the presence of God with you. Remember Ephesians 3:17 "Christ will make His home in your hearts as you trust in Him. Your roots will grow down into God's love and keep you strong." As we make our pilgrimage to special places and spaces, heart-warming memories can inspire and nourish us. "Don't be dejected and sad, for the joy of the Lord is your strength!" (Nehemiah 8:10)

What is life without my love?

Visiting those spaces and places of cherished memory can inspire us in our onward journey through life, and to the dawn of the Eternal Day.

For Reflection.

There are a host of views about the issue of memorials and there is really no right or wrong way to do it.

Does having a place to visit bring you some comfort? Is it helpful to have a physical space where remembrance can be focused?

Can the care of a memorial become a pressure and a problem?

Does it matter if the time comes when you are not able to look after it in the way you would like?

Do you feel that a space has more merit than a place? Maybe a tree; a shared sea view; a country park; more so than a marble inscription; a memorial stone or a place to display flowers?

Maybe it is both?

Or neither?

Billy Graham was once walking through the Senators Dining Room in Washington DC and a Senator stopped him and said, "Hey Billy we are just having a discussion about pessimism and optimism. Which are you?" He replied with a smile, "I'm an optimist." "Why?" They asked. "Because I've read the last chapter of the Bible," was Billy's response.

We carry our memories with us. Our loved ones don't wave to us from the past but beckon to us from the future. We look forward to the final chapter which is to be reunited in our new eternal home.

Do you feel affirmed and encouraged by that prospect?

11

A CHANGE OF IDENTITY

It is a strange thing when you meet up with an old friend after almost a whole life time. Barry had been head-boy in our Cathedral High School; he was confident, cheerful, popular and capable which made him a perfect fit for the role. Fifty years on from school we met again having renewed contact through Facebook. We had an easy and lively conversation about school days; school productions in which we both played a part; teachers – good; bad and indifferent; there was a host of memories.

It was also a mutual reassessment of identity; I had only ever known him as head-boy but now he had become so much more; husband, Father and Grandfather. I discovered that he had spent most of his working life in Malawi where his engineering expertise had taken him and where he had, for many years, headed up the transport system keeping the country interconnected. He had fallen in love with Africa and his burgeoning artistic talent had grown while painting the flora, fauna and animal life of his adopted country. He had captured the light shade and beauty of his beloved Africa on canvas. I looked across the table at the man of 70 as I remembered the boy of 16. No longer head-boy, he had a multifaceted identity that had weighty and wonderful aspects to it. It was hard to take in at one sitting but of course, for him it had been the passage of a lifetime.

One of the strongest and most joyous aspects of my identity for 44 years had been that of husband to Barbara. I loved that identity. Sometimes I would hear Barbs talking to a friend or colleague and I picked up the phrase, "My Ian." I loved being called "My Ian" by her, it gave me a sense of inner pride. I was glad to be 'her Ian.' I also loved being Rector of All Saints Aston with Ulley and Swallownest. I can't deny that there is a certain frisson in the status of Rector. It is an historic role dating from the 12th century and all the names of Rectors are recorded and remembered on a framed list, beautifully written in script, that hangs on the wall below the Bell Tower. My name is among them. Part of me wonders how a Geordie boy, born in a humble council house, end up on such an illustrious list! In all honesty though, I believe my greatest joy about being Rector of Aston was not about status but service. I was priest and pastor to a lovely community and I never ceased to appreciate that privilege.

Retirement was a new kind of bereavement; I was leaving my beloved church and community and moving to the other side of the city. I had thought I would attend the Deanery Chapter meeting in my new area, but a fellow retired clergyman told me, "Don't try to attend the Chapter meeting there, retired clergy are not welcome." I was really surprised by that because retired clergy had been welcome and valued in my previous deanery. I emailed the Area Dean and quoted this friend. The Area Dean replied, "I don't know where he gets his ideas from. The truth is. retired clergy are neither welcome nor unwelcome." That seemed even worse to me as it seemed to say, "We are totally indifferent – your presence or absence has no significance - it really doesn't matter whether you attend or not. We will lose nothing if you don't attend and we will gain nothing if you do." Maybe I was being super-sensitive having just lost my wife, but this made me feel a loss of identity; diminished and invisible and reinforced my sense of bereavement. It is easy to feel diminished by a loss of identity.

On July 11th 2016 I lost my identity as a husband and gained a new one that I detested – widower. It was a surreal moment the first time I filled in a form that required me to designate myself as 'Widower.' "Is that me?" I thought, "Does that word describe my status and define my experience now?" I know many people who have grappled with the strangeness of widowhood. At that point you have to make a decision about yourself. 'Who am I now that my love is dead?' That is a question to be tackled and sometimes to be wrestled with. I think it is all too easy to don the widow's weeds of this new identity and shrink into this new role. That is a sad spectacle – to embrace widowhood as if this is now who you are is a downward spiral. We are so much more than our loss. We are not defined by our bereavement.

I was once in a church house group and the leader asked us to share what we were most proud of and that gave us the most satisfaction in our lives. A guy called Paul jumped in first and said, "I won a certificate for the quality of my woodwork in carpentry class at school. That was the proudest moment of my life." We all looked at his lovely wife and his bright eyed 12-year-old son and in one spontaneous voice said, "Really!! Woodwork certificate!!" His mind had slipped back to that moment which clearly was important to 13-year-old Paul. But he had bypassed the truly wonderful in his life and lighted upon the trivial. His wife and son looked a bit crestfallen. In examining our identity, we shouldn't fall into the trap of bypassing what is truly great in our lives and accepting a lesser identity. In our journey of recovery through the bleak days of grief we really need to know who we truly are.

One thing I returned to again and again after Barbaras death was my enduring identity as a follower of Jesus. I remembered an acquaintance who is an outstanding theologian. He is brilliant academically. He has several degrees and a Ph.D from Harvard. Yet on his study wall you will find only his faded baptismal certificate which has pride of place. Nothing else. It reminds him that his primary identity is 'follower of Jesus.' Nothing else really matters in the end.

Quite a few years ago Ian Smael (Ishmael) wrote a song called "Father God I wonder how I managed to exist without the knowledge of your faithfulness and your loving care." When he first wrote that song it included the line, "now I am your son, I am adopted in your family." At Spring Harvest my nephew, Sam went along to an event that was an audience with Ishmael – he was singing his songs and answering questions from the young people. My nephew, Sam was a young teenager at the time and he asked a question about this song. He said, "Why did you write, 'Now I am your son...' God has daughters too. Surely it should be inclusive." Ishmael agreed and said, "When I wrote it it was my spontaneous song to God. It was deeply personal and expressed my heart felt appreciation of Gods love for me. I never anticipated an audience singing it. It was just about me and God – and that's who I am – His son."

I think that we need to rediscover that identity in processing our grief. The first and foremost thing is that you are is a follower of Jesus; a deeply loved child of God. He could not love you more and he will not love you less. You are utterly and completely loved by the God who is love.

My wife and I only ever attended one professional football match together. It was one of the things we were planning to do more of in retirement but we never got the chance. The one match we did attend was at Bramall Lane, Sheffield and it was Sheffield United versus Colchester United. Our children Paul and Sarah are both adopted and when Paul was 22 his biological family reached out to us to ask if he would be willing for contact to be established. That was the beginning of a new journey for him. We all had some trepidation but it worked out really well. Among the many things he discovered was that his biological cousin was a professional footballer and was goalkeeper for Colchester United at that time. So Barbs and I attended that match largely to see Dean perform in goal and he kindly secured complimentary tickets for us. This meant that we were sitting with the Colchester fans behind the goal. They were the truly enthusiastic, hardcore fans and when they sang "Stand up if you love Cole U," we stood up and raised our hands like the rest!

What amused me most was when the Sheffield United team came on the Colchester fans pointed and chanted, "Who are ya?! Who are ya?!" It is another way of saying, "We don't recognise that you have any significance, value or prestige." But of course, that wouldn't make such a good football chant. "Who are ya!?" says it all. It is a good question for us to ask ourselves, not to disrespect ourselves but to find ourselves. It is a fundamental question when you have lost your nearest and dearest and you feel half of you has gone. Who am I now? The truth is that you are a completely cherished child of God. That is your true identity.

In your grief you need to rediscover this utterly astonishing reality that God deeply loves you and delights to call you his child. Chris Tomlinson wrote a worship song called, 'Good, Good Father,' that simply and beautifully conveys this thought of how much we are loved by Father God:

Oh, I've heard a thousand stories
Of what they think your like
But I've heard the tender whisper
Of love in the dead of night
And you tell me that's you're pleased
And that I'm never alone

You're a good good Father
It's who you are
It's who you are
It's who you are
And I'm loved by You
It's who I am
It's who I am
It's who I am.

During the last year of his life David Watson wrote a book called 'Fear No Evil.' It was about his personal struggle with terminal cancer. Chapter 9 of that book is entitled "Enjoying God." That seems like a difficult concept during life's final, painful, journey. Yet he is speaking from his own experience of enjoying God. He writes, "The most common word for worship in the Bible comes sixty-six times. It could be translated, 'I come towards to kiss.' God is love and he wants us to respond to him in love... People today need to know that God loves them as individuals, just as they are with all their faults and failings. Comparatively few know deep down within their hearts, that God really loves them, more than they could ever begin to imagine. However, when we 'come towards to kiss' by opening our hearts to Him in worship, we are able to receive his love poured into our hearts by the Holy Spirit. (Romans 5:5) We need to find God's love and stay resting in it. Nothing is more important than that."

Who are you? You are God's child, completely enveloped in God's love. This is not about a sterile religious adherence but rather a personal and intimate relationship of love with our loving Heavenly Father. That is the identity we need to deepen and develop in our days of grief and loss. Nothing is more important.

What is life without my love?

Bereavement may have mounted a serious attack on your sense identity but when life takes everything from you God can become everything to you and bring you back to your true identity as his cherished child.

That is who you are.

For Reflection.

Who do you think you are?

Has your own sense of identity been affected by your bereavement?

The term 'Widow or Widower' may now define your status, how do you feel about it? Is it an unwelcome title or an image to hide behind?

We may have many roles in life; parent; grandparent; friend; group member; worshipper; worker; senior citizen; customer; walker; runner; client – the list is endless. But the variety of roles we play do not define us.

What does define you; what is your defining identity?

St Peter writes (1 Peter 2:9) **...*you are God's special possession* ...** and what is true for God's family is true for God's children.

Is that who you are? God's special possession?

How does that play out in your daily life?

12

GRIEF IN A TIME OF ISOLATION

I am writing this in the time of Corona Virus Lockdown. It's is a desperately difficult time in so many ways. What a time to experience bereavement and endure life in isolation alone without your spouse. The last funeral I conducted was for Christine who had been a very committed member of the church where I used to be Vicar, St. Cuthbert's, Fir Vale, Sheffield. Christine ran the Parents and Toddlers Group for almost 20 years there. Her husband Jeff had recently retired and they had been looking forward to spending more time together and had lots of plans. Jeff went to visit his very elderly Mother in Surrey for the weekend while Christine stayed at home. On the Sunday afternoon their son Simon called on his Mum while Jeff was still away and, tragically found her dead in the back garden of their home. She had not been ill so her sudden death was deeply shocking. It was a privilege to conduct Christine's funeral. I saw Jeff twice after the funeral for coffee, catch-up and prayer and then we were instructed to self-isolate because of the virus. Two months before Jeff and Christine had been sharing a full and active life together and now he is in lonely self-isolation. That is a tough call; a deeply challenging time.

Her Majesty the Queen broadcast an Easter message in 2020. We are used to hearing her at Christmas, but in her 68-year reign this was her first Easter message. Her Christian faith shone through her words when she said, "We need Easter as much as ever.... As dark as death can be - particularly for those suffering with grief – light and life are greater." When you are grappling with the raw reality of grief in a time of isolation, holding on to the hope of resurrection is hugely important. To live with the irrepressible hope that 'light and life are greater than the darkness of death' requires inner resources to draw upon and a resilience of spirit which is rooted and grounded in God.

John Donne expresses a profound and ageless truth in his poem, 'No man is an Island.'

No man is an island,
Entire of itself.
Each is a piece of the continent,
A part of the main.
If a clod be washed away by the sea,
Europe is the less.
As well as if a promontory were.
As well as if a manor of thine own
Or of thy friends were.
Each man's death diminishes me,
For I am involved in mankind.
Therefore, send not to know
For whom the bell tolls,
It tolls for thee.

Human beings do not thrive when isolated from others. Enforced isolation is a tough call for everyone, but perhaps it has a particular poignancy for those who are grieving the death of their life partner. There are huge mental health implications for this period of isolation so our hope and prayer must be that it will be over before too much time has elapsed. We are social creatures and it is clear that this experience has brought out the best in many who have been reaching out through social media. 'When we are no longer able to change our situation, we are challenged to change ourselves.' Many are doing that and are trying their best to look after themselves and each other. Even in times of coronavirus we are finding ways of reaching beyond our own small island of isolation.

Some practical strategies are proving important in isolation. I first met Tony in the bereavement group that I attended after the death of my wife. Tony was grieving the death of his wife also. The group proved to be a place of mutual care and support. It was in that group that Tony met Sandra who was mourning the death of her husband. A real friendship sprang up between them which eventually deepened into love. Both were open and caring people and it was lovely to see that they had found each other. They were part of a wider group of friends who had developed into a network of mutual care. Everyone could see how much they loved one another and was pleased that through the dark times of bereavement, the light was shining again for them and they were able to share the journey of life together.

I didn't see quite so much of the group once my ministry

took me to St. Mary's Denham, but I did keep in touch and received texts and phone calls from Tony and Sandra. Then I heard Sandra was unwell; back pain which turned out to be a rapidly advancing cancer of the spine. Her last text to me said, "These things come to try us, but I will stay positive and hopefully get through this challenge.' But she didn't get through it, its advance was very rapid and she died just days later. Tony faced the grim reality of grief once again. He and the family asked me to conduct the funeral service. It was not easy; Sandra was such a people person; full of life and Tony looked so crushed and desolate. Friends rallied round him and long walks with his good friend, Roy, helped. Then came 'lockdown.'

Tony struggled, but established patterns of structure to ease him through each day. He told me of his efforts in the garden, of his decorating the kitchen and hall of his home: keeping busy helped. The other thing which helped was a communal initiative. He lives in a cul-de-sac and he received an invitation to bring a chair with him to the end of the cul-de-sac where the road widens out into a big circle. At an appointed time, he and his neighbours meet; sitting in a circle 3 metres apart from one another. They do this three times a week and are punctilious about social distancing. This is proving a life-saver for Tony. He has lived there for 42 years but in these weeks of self-isolation he has got to know people he has never known before. His neighbours know of his loss and are empathetic and supportive. It is a strange and wonderful phenomenon that in these trying days, people are coming closer to one another from a distance, finding ways of leaving their island of isolation and reconnecting as human beings.

The other thing that I have observed and experienced is

that the jagged edges of grief that had become less barbed with the passing of time seem to have regained some of their capacity to wound. Because we now live in a kind of vacuum and routine is disrupted, there is much more opportunity of being alone with our thoughts and those thoughts often lead us back into the shadows.

Three weeks into lockdown I received an email from a friend whose wife had died 3 years ago. He wrote, "Since lockdown I have been stuck in this vacuum of isolation, missing regular activities and meeting up with family and friends, I find myself distracted with thoughts of the past – I see spring on its way, the trees, shrubs and flowers in bud and some in full flower and I think, 'Jackie loved that one and the scent of this one. Everything speaks to me of Jackie. Using kitchen utensils reminds me of her at work in the kitchen, just using the same items. If I go for a walk, I think of her shoes treading the same path. Am I different from others in this respect? Is it just lockdown or am I still grieving? Sometimes I feel it could drive me crazy!" John is a strong, well balanced human being but the present circumstances have reignited the glowing embers of his grief and in his solitude he is involuntarily revisiting former memories he thought he had left behind. It reminded me of the verse from Elizabeth Jennings:

> Time does not heal,
> It makes a half-stitched scar
> That can be broken and you feel
> Grief as total as in the first hour.

Trish, a friend whose husband died 17 months ago and who read my book, "By a Departing Light'. referred to chapter 3 entitled, "Choose Life." She said, "I did choose life - I know that is what Bill would want me to do, but now I can't choose living!" She feels life is constricted by the virus; she can't hug her grandchildren; she can't be there to celebrate their birthdays: all desperately upsetting - her grief has resurfaced and her heart aches at times. Many, who thought they were in the process of healing, have now had their 'half-stitched scar' broken again.

Like many friends of mine, I too am longing to hug those dear to me; especially my family. It is a kind of yearning in the midst of this so-called 'lock down.' People of my age category and degree of vulnerability can no longer see our loved ones except on Face Time, or Zoom, or some other online platform and, whilst that is hugely valuable, it is no substitute for a hug; a virtual hug just doesn't do the job!

Some people like to be very touchy-freely whilst others seem happy to remain aloof and are apparently at ease in a touch free world. Not me!

On my first Sunday morning as Rector of Aston, whilst I was conducting the service, a voice rang out clearly, 'The new Rector's got very shiny shoes." The voice belonged to a 90-year-old worshipper who was very deaf and didn't know how to modulate her volume. Over the months and years that followed I got to know her and found her austere, sometimes difficult and judgmental, but underneath her hard shell I sometimes caught glimpses of a lovely human being. She told me one day, with some pride, that she had never held a baby in all her 90 years. When I asked if she had ever wanted to she held herself stiffly and with disdain saying firmly "No, never!"

I believe deprivation had left its mark upon her and that her hard shell was a kind of self-protection. For the truth is, we human beings long for human touch and there is no longing more primal, and no experience more soul stirring, than that of holding a baby or hugging a child. As I write this, I know countless Grandparents who are feeling a kind of starvation – a hunger to hug their grandchildren. The truth is, we humans are wired for touch and a need for physical contact remains until the day we die. I hadn't really thought about it before but this enforced isolation has made me deeply aware of my need to hug and be hugged in return.

There was a sad story on Today, the Radio 4 news programme this week. Hannah and John had been married for almost 43 years but they had both contracted Corona Virus. Hannah improved but John's condition worsened and he was taken to Hospital. He died one day before their forty third Wedding Anniversary. Hannah spoke with sadness of the fact that for the last week of his life, none of the family could be with John. "Everyone was wonderful," she said. "My family, my church, the Hospital - but nothing can alter the fact that we couldn't be together while he was dying, and now I am alone here and no one can give me a hug," she said, her tears evident. It was no trivial matter. The need for a hug is fundamental to us as human beings. Dr Terry Kupers, Psychologist and author writes, "Physical contact is a requirement of being human. There is something healing about touch. It is not just correlated to being human – it is being human."

At the time of writing there is no way of knowing how long 'lockdown' will last. Still fewer of us know when, or if, life will return to normal.

We always need to build hope into our lives so that we can find a way through, when anxiety threatens to engulf us. This virus crisis is such a time, but there are other times in our lives when we need the buoyancy of a lively hope, that is much more than wishful thinking. President Obama wrote an autobiographical book called, "The Audacity of Hope." He clearly described his journey to faith in Christ in that book and his idea of audacious hope means even when circumstances are far from promising, yet hope will still arise undefeated and undefeatable.

Yet there is more to hope than audacity, good though that is. I also heard the expression, "The defiance of hope" from Canon Giles Fraser when speaking about the coronavirus from a Christian perspective, which I thought was helpful; but there is more to hope than defiance also. St Paul writing in Romans 15:13 says, "May the God of hope fill you with all joy and peace as you trust in Him, so that you may overflow with hope by the power of the Holy Spirit."

Patrick Regan writing in his book, When Faith Gets Shaken describes a very dark and difficult time that he and his wife were undergoing. They were desperate, stressed and broken and couldn't see the way ahead. He writes, "My wife, Diana and I both felt at a loss for how to cope. At one particularly bleak moment she stepped out of the room to take a minute on her own to cry out to God. She told him it was too hard and that she couldn't do it anymore. As she prayed she saw a picture of a tunnel and immediately thought of the phrase, 'the light at the end of the tunnel.' But as she looked she couldn't see any light in the distance; the tunnel looked too long. As she looked again she saw the light was all round her, at the start of the tunnel not at the end. In that moment she knew God had given her our survival strategy to get us through the difficult months ahead: we had to be fully present in the moment. We couldn't look to how life would be in a day, a week, a month or a year; if we looked ahead waiting for the light, we'd miss the fact that God was already with us, right where we stood. Over the last year I learned about real courage, peace, anger, guilt, surrender, hope and God's love."

This Corona crisis is a bit like a tunnel and, at present, it is hard to see the light at the end, but through the presence of the God of Hope the light is with us in the moment. The light of hope illuminates our way each day. It's tough but living hope sustains us and in the words of our Queen;
"as dark as death can be … light and life are greater."

What is life without my love?

In a time of isolation, it is undeniably hard, but in each moment we can 'overflow with hope by the power of the Holy Spirit.'

Hope wins in the end.

Time for Reflection

What resources did you find in your experience of lockdown?

Did you, and do you, feel held by God through the crisis of Covid 19?

Is there any antidote to the encroachment of loneliness?

George MacDonald wrote; "I have never been by any means a book-worm; but the very outside of a book had a charm to me. It was a kind of sacrament – an outward and visible sign of an inward and spiritual grace as, indeed, what on God's earth isn't?"

Did you find books a blessing in lockdown?

Are they part of your self-nurture?

How important is it to have the Bible as part of your daily routine?

George's MacDonald found everything *on God's earth a sacrament.*

Did you see the glory of God in creation during your lockdown experience?

Did the colours seem more vivid and the beauty of creation more glorious?

Is there a place for looking and listening for God is a daily, silent, prayerful awareness that can help us through loss and loneliness?

Even in dark days can you feel the buoyancy of hope?

May the God of hope fill you with all joy and peace as you trust in him, so that you may overflow with hope by the power of the Holy Spirit.

Romans 15:13

13

GONE TOO SOON

On many occasions as a minister I have visited an elderly bereaved person whose husband or wife has died, and I have been surprised by how much they apologised for their tears. They would say something like, "I'm so sorry, I really shouldn't be crying like this. We were married for fifty-five years and had a lovely life together, so I should be grateful."

My response to that would be, "Don't apologise for your tears - if anyone has the right to cry it's you. Of course you're grateful, but now there is a huge hollow. Because you have had a long and happy marriage, it doesn't make it any easier to say goodbye; in some ways it makes it harder."

Words of comfort are hard to find when a life has been cruelly cut short and tears are of heartbreak, shock and bewilderment. I remember going to see Michael after his young wife, Tracey, had died. He talked and wept - sometimes breaking into sobs mid-sentence. I had known them both since they were teenagers; they were so right together. Both their families had been members of the church where I had been minister when I first came to Sheffield in 1989. I remember seeing their teenage friendship blossom into love and thinking how perfect they seemed for one another; and they were. I was delighted to reconnect with them as Rector of Aston, because their two beautiful daughters were pupils in our All Saints Church School.

During 2013, Tracey had started to experience some health problems. A cyst had been diagnosed, but that cyst had turned out to be stage 4 ovarian cancer. Though this news was devastating, they had drawn upon their resources of faith, believed their prayer would be answered and Tracey would not die. Both their families were people of strong Christian faith and they, along with their church, all stood together in prayer for healing. I visited Tracey in Weston Park Hospital and was genuinely surprised at how upbeat she was. She looked at me very intently and said, "Please pray for me. I need a miracle otherwise I'm not going to make it." I sat with her and prayed for healing. She said a firm and clear "Amen" when I finished, and her face broke into a broad smile as if confident that the miracle was on the way. Neither Michael nor Tracey accepted that she was going to die, but in fact there was only three months between her diagnosis and death.

Two weeks before she died, Tracey had a serious talk with Michael about the future. She said, "If I die I want you to remarry. You will need a wife and the girls will need a Mum." She was quite matter of fact, but clear and positive. She told her parents this was her wish when they visited the hospital. Michael realised later she was letting go bravely and graciously. He felt she was giving him permission to live his future life as fully as possible; it was her loving and gracious gift to him. Both their hearts were breaking but Tracey turned Michael's face towards life, as she turned her own towards death.

Of course, both had the sustaining assurance of Christian hope as the foundation of their lives, but that does not remove or relieve the searing pain of loss. They were living through an experience of stress and trauma which no words are adequate to describe.

Michael and Tracey's daughters, Heidi and Florence were only 6 and 8, and did all they could to protect them from the impact of Tracey's illness. But of course, in the end, they couldn't protect them from the trauma and tragedy of the death of their darling Mum.

One the day of Tracy's death Michael came straight from the Hospital to school to break the news to Heidi and Florence. Fortunately he met the Headteacher, Sue Mellor, an outstanding Headteacher, both professionally and pastorally, and she proved to be a great support to him. She invited him to use her office to break the news, which he was glad to accept. He felt he needed a warm and welcoming space, not some sanitised "room of doom'. Michael told them in the most straightforward fashion, without equivocation; he held them and said, "Mummy died today." They cried together.

I once attended a course with other Prison Chaplains about how to break the news of a death. Many scenarios were discussed, but the essential point was never avoid the word death or dead when breaking the most unwelcome news. It reminded me of an interview in which Michael Aspel asked Mel Brookes, "I understand that you have lost your Father."

"That's not true," said Mel, "We didn't lose him; he died. Do you think we wouldn't go out looking for him if he was just lost?" The audience laughed and Aspel realised he had been set up. Before the show Mel Brookes said, "I recently lost my Dad; ask me about that." So he did in the precise words that Mel Brookes put into his mind.

Simplicity, honesty and humanity are called for when breaking the news of the death of a loved one, and never more so than when breaking that devastating news to a child. Michael and his two girls cried for Tracey and hugged one another then, as they prepared to go home, Heidi asked, with the beautiful naivety of a child, "Please can I have Mummy's shoes?" Perhaps uncomplicated naivety is a child's way of coping with the devastating grief of a parent's death. Those girls had no real idea of what lay ahead, but Michael tried to provide them with structural normality to help them process their grief and engage with life. They cried that night, then returned to school the following day; only ever having one day off. They had the support of two loving sets of grandparents as well as the support of Sue, the Headteacher, and their teachers. Sue's office became a refuge for them over the following months. During break times they could come and bring a friend each with them and Sue left them drawing and colouring materials to use. They would sit and chat and draw and make things together. It became their place of safety to retreat to when they needed it during the school day.

Michael and Tracey did not just have a good marriage, they had a great marriage, one of those, 'heirs together of the grace of life' partnerships. They were each other's world, talking endlessly as best friends will. Some summer evenings, sitting on the patio, they would talk and laugh until the wee small hours, losing all track of time.

Michael is a strong person and, for the sake of his girls, maintained structures of normality after Tracey's death, providing a safe and loving space for them to feel secure. But the pain and anguish of grief was an ever-present reality in those early days of loss. Simon Thomas, (former Blue Peter Presenter) describes the all-consuming sense of loss graphically in his book, Love Interrupted. After Gemma's untimely death he wrote,
"How can I put into words the emotions I felt at quarter to six on that Friday in November? I felt like a huge bomb had just exploded and we were at the epicentre. The blast was so shocking and so intense that it left us feeling totally numb. The pain and devastation couldn't even begin to register, I was totally and utterly bewildered. After those endless, exhausting hours of hoping and praying that Gemma would somehow pull through, and the reality of saying goodbye, there was nothing but a sense of profound emptiness. As we stood around her bed, everything felt so utterly quiet. In that moment the rest of the world no longer existed. In the place of her laboured breathing there were tears for those she had left behind".

One thing unusual about Michael's way of handling his grief, was that he did not feel angry. Anger of a typical response to bereavement. Simon Thomas felt a sense of rage at the injustice of Gemma's death aged only 40. Similarly, the character played by Ricky Gervais in 'After Life,' certainly felt angry; it was his primary emotion in those months following his wife's death. It is often part of the experience of loss. However, we all process our grief in slightly different ways and Michael did not experience anger, instead accepting what he knew he could not refuse to accept, the death of his beautiful Tracey.

Sue Mellor said of Michael following Tracey's death, "I never saw anger in Michael just profound sadness and I was, and still am, in awe at how he coped. He had a sheer determination to make everything right for Florence and Heidi - they were his reason for living." The question he asked himself was, "What is the best reaction to this?" He knew in his heart anger was pointless and he must find more productive ways to channel his energy. For three months he went to a Cruse bereavement counsellor who said, with some surprise, "You are the most open person I have ever met in your circumstances." Michael knew that anger was pointless and he had so many challenges of his own to face, he knew he would need all his positive energy to cope. He became the highest performing sales consultant in the UK for his Company and he excelled at being a great Dad. He had meltdowns and breakdowns and needed and received help, but somehow he maintained his focus.

Before Tracey's death, Michael had been part of the church prayer team, which involved encouraging others to pray for a whole litany of needs, as well as praying himself. Now, 6 years on from Tracey's death, I asked him about his prayer life. He said, 'My Christianity is different now - I am completely clueless about God's plan and I accept now I may never know. The one thing I asked God for he either wouldn't or couldn't help me with. That has changed my prayer life. I can't pray for everyday needs in the way that I used to, yet I still pray with my children every night and our focus is gratitude."

He went on to explain the deep sense of thankfulness, "I am grateful for my fantastic marriage; we had a wonderful relationship and I thank God for all that my life with Tracey has given me including our two wonderful daughters. Life is good and I am grateful. That is my focus of prayer."

I so appreciate Michael's honesty and clarity on the issue of prayer. Choosing gratitude in the face of deep sorrow; making thanksgiving the heartfelt response is the hard choice, but the healing choice. And it really is a choice.

During the summer of 2015, Barbara and I spent many afternoons driving around the Derbyshire Peak District which we were fortunate to have on our doorstep. We had been in the habit of doing weekly 10 – 15 mile walks but because of Barbara's illness, that was no longer possible. We could still take in the stunning beauty of the Peaks from the car, however. We would play some worship CDs on the car stereo as we drove and our favourite became Matt Redman's "Blessed be the name of the Lord." The second verse is:

Blessed be Your name
On the road marked with suffering,
Though there's pain in the offering
Blessed be Your name.

Then the bridge:

You give and take away
You give and take away
My heart will choose to say
Lord blessed be Your name.

Those words are drawn from Job; "The Lord gave, the Lord has taken away, blessed be the name of the Lord." I glanced across at Barbara one afternoon as these words were being sung and her eyes were brimming with tears. She was 'on the road marked with suffering and there was pain in the offering'. It was no easy thing then to choose to say, 'Blessed be the name of the Lord.'

Michael has chosen to live gratefully rather than grudgingly and that shines through. There is no one else in his life at present, although he has dated twice. "Tracey was an absolute gift," he says, "I know I won't find another Tracey but I'm confident that I will find a new gift, a new fantastic future, and Tracey wanted that for me."

What Michael has learned through his loss and his journey of grief, is that his understanding of life was too small. He said his vision was linear and based on his own expectations. Everything had been thrown in the air when Tracey died and when he had picked himself up from that massive body blow, he found that life was a lot bigger than he had conceived; his vision expanded.

He discovered some words of Mother Teresa gave him a foundation for a life of purpose;

"People are often unreasonable and self-centred;
Forgiven them anyway.
If you are kind people may accuse you of ulterior motives;
Be kind anyway.
If you are honest people may cheat you;
Be honest anyway.
If you find happiness people may be jealous;
Be happy anyway.
The good you do may be forgotten tomorrow;
Do good anyway.
Give the world the best you can and it may never be enough;

Give your best anyway,
For you see, in the end it is between you and God.
It was never between you and them anyway."

It is an inspiring vision of life; the right way to live without a self-centred agenda. In the midst of his devastating loss Michael has learned some hugely important lessons for life; he has chosen to live with the grace of gratitude; he has expanded his vision to take in the multifaceted nature of the amazing gift of life and he lives humbly, trustingly, gratefully and with integrity. I think of something else Mother Teresa said which applies to him,

"Life is a song, sing it. Life is a struggle, accept it."

In the massive blow of Tracey's death, life undoubtedly became a struggle; yet in embracing the gift of life with its awesome potential, his heart is in tune with the melody and music which life offers.

Recently I had a Zoom conversation with Michael to talk through these issues. He talks swiftly and fluently, yet six years after Tracey's death his voice still breaks with emotion, and tears flow as he speaks of her. But in the midst of his pain, he has discovered potential and opened his eyes to the wondrous gift of life.

What is life without my young Love?
Devastated but not destroyed.
Stalled but not stifled.
Crushed but not broken.

There is still the bright light of hope which beckons and if we choose the path of gratitude, we can find life is still full of purpose and potential.

"My heart will choose to say ……?"
For Reflection

The striking thing about the story of Michael in his loss of Tracey is his rejection of anger and his embrace of purpose.

We often get sidetracked down the dead end street of anger.

How can we resist that temptation?

Can anger be resisted or should we go with it?

Does anger have a place and a purpose?

Paul writes is Ephesians 5:26. **Be angry, yet do not sin. Do not let the sun go down on your anger.** Paul is saying 'don't act upon your anger; don't hold on to anger.'

Is there a way of redirecting that energy towards purpose; refocusing on the good?

Maybe Michael's focus on thankfulness provides us with an answer to anger.

Can we choose to live with the grace of gratitude?

Psalm 34:1 The Psalmist writes, *I will bless the Lord at all times; his praise shall continually be in my mouth.*

Though we are living with loss can we still make that choice?

14

HOME

When my Father was approaching his 90th birthday, he was suddenly taken ill with pneumonia and taken into Hospital. He made a slow recovery but picked up an infection and had further complications. My sister and I knew that Dad's wife, our step Mum, Mollie, could no longer give him the care he needed at home. He had progressively lost mobility and was now in a very needy state; so we began to look for a suitable care home for him. One afternoon when I was sitting at his hospital bed he said, "I want to go home."

I replied, "I know that Dad but you do understand that Mollie can't look after you, don't you?" He looked at me with a little smile, "I don't mean the bungalow," he said, and pointed upwards, "I mean Home! My true Home!" Then he added, "I won't make it to my 90th birthday: I'll be Home by then." And he was. In fact we held his funeral on his 90th birthday.

That vision of going 'Home' when our earthly journey is

done can be a comfort to those who are stepping out of this life as well as those they are leaving behind. John Chapter 14 : 1-6 is often read at funerals. There Jesus speaks of 'My Father's house' as a place where there are many rooms and tells us clearly that He is 'preparing a place for us and will come again to receive us to Himself.' His description, "My Father's House" conjures up for us a reassuring picture of "Home."

When I began my ministry in Doncaster as Assistant Minister I was a young man of 22 and I stayed with two lovely families for the first year; six months with each. The first family was the Schofields who welcomed me and treated me like a son, as did the second, the Jones; both families were loving and caring. In particular, Ethel Jones was a radiant Christian who was full of love.

I kept in touch with both of those families down through the years; more particularly the Jones', as my sister in law, Pauline, married their son, David. When Ethel approached death, she did so not simply with acceptance, but with joy. She planned her own funeral service which she called; "My Home Going Service,' and that title appeared on the front of the service sheet. Ethel Jones demonstrated a complete, unhindered joy in going Home.

Of course, belief in heaven can be difficult when you're wrestling with doubts and living through darkness. When Simon Thomas was at Gemma's bedside in those last desperate moments of her life, although he was uncertain she could hear him, he made her this promise, "I promised her I would not return to the drink and that I would not give up on my faith." But he went on to say, "But when the intensity of my grief hit home, those promises confronted me with two of the biggest battles I had to face." About a year after Gemma's death, feeling a deep sense of loneliness, he describes looking up at the stars wondering ...

'Is Gemma really in heaven? Does heaven actually exist? What if it doesn't? What if it's just a crutch we've invented to soften the devastating blow of death?'

It is perfectly normal to have such questions when living with grief. Doubt is not the opposite of faith it is actually part of faith. The Bible paints heaven in broad brush strokes. The Book of Revelation focuses on Heaven's riches:

"Each of the 12 foundations was a precious stone. The first was jasper, the second was sapphire, the third was agate, the fourth was emerald, the fifth was onyx, the sixth was carnelian, the seventh was chrysolite, the eighth was beryl, the ninth was topaz, the tenth was chrysoprase, the eleventh was jacinth and the twelfth was amethyst. Each of the twelve gates was a solid pearl. The streets of the city were made of pure gold, clear as crystal."
(Revelation 21:18-21)

It is an extraordinary catalogue and begs the question, are these semi-precious stones realistic construction materials? I suspect not. The writer is giving us a picture of a city bursting with colour and shimmering with fantastical radiance; so glorious it is beyond the human mind to conceive.

It brings to mind Paul's words in 1 Corinthians 2:9 ...

" No eye has seen, nor ear heard, no heart has imagined, what God has prepared for those who love him."

I was brought up on the 'streets of gold' imagery of heaven and children are very literal in their vision. We used to sing a chorus in Sunday school called 'Heaven is better than this.' It contained the line, 'walking on the streets of solid gold; living in a land where we never grow old.' My Sunday school teacher was called George Mayhew. I loved him as a little boy; he seemed to me exactly what a Christian is meant to be. He always greeted me with a warm smile and I could tell he was genuinely pleased to see me -and, in turn, I was always delighted to see him. One Sunday I asked him what had become for me a burning question about heaven. "Will we be able to play football in heaven. Do they have footballs there?"

He replied, "No I don't think they do have footballs in heaven, but they have grapes the size of footballs. Perhaps you could get a few of the lads together and play football with one of the grapes!"

That was a deeply unsatisfactory answer to my question. I had a mental picture of my foot sinking into grape pulp up to the ankle. It wasn't going to work and it certainly put a dampener on my idea of heaven!

Literalism should be avoided when contemplating heaven. When I was invited by the consultant into a hospital ward side-room for a conversation following a further scan on my wife's brain, my heart sank. I knew the news was not going to be good. He said, "I'm sorry to say your wife has only months to live?"

"Can you be precise about how many months?" I asked.

He gave me his honest assessment; "Maybe as few as three but not more than six." She actually lived a further four months.

I asked him to tell me what to expect from the process of dying. I knew Barbara would ask me that. He said, "Towards the end she will sleep a lot and then, finally, she won't wake up."

I remember the expression on Barbara's face when I told her what the consultant had said. It was a look of the most profound sadness. She was pensive as she processed the information. She shed no tears but she asked, as I knew she would, "What will happen; what will my death be like?"

I repeated what the consultant had told me, "You will sleep a lot towards the end and finally fall asleep and not wake up. You will slip peacefully away. The next time you wake you will be in heaven." She nodded slowly and sighed deeply, an air of resignation in her manner; the idea of her final sleep seemed to comfort her.

When I became Rector at Aston I discovered Sunday evening services alternated between Evensong and Compline; both choral and both beautiful. Compline is a service of prayers at the end of the day. The English word Compline comes from the Latin completorium - work is over, day is done and all is complete. I loved our service of Compline at All Saints, the music was written and arranged by our own Musical Director, Paul Hudson and was beautifully reflective. The service begins with the brief prayer;

The Lord Almighty grant us a quiet night and a perfect end. It concludes with; Save us O Lord, while waking, and guard us while sleeping, that awake we may watch with Christ, and asleep may rest in peace.

I usually walked home afterwards through the stillness of twilight wrapped in a palpable sense of peace. I often found myself reflecting of life's little day as I walked home and pondered the fact that dying well involves a kind of compline – rest beckons; work is done and peace prevails. The words of Simeon in the Nunc dimittis are always part of Compline;

Now let your servant go in peace.

In his book, Dying Well, John Wyatt expresses this thought clearly. He talks about the fact that even faithful Christians are fearful of the process of dying, they worry,

"Will I be struggling to breathe, experiencing unbearable agony, overwhelmed with fear, sucked into a terrifying black hole of non-existence? It is easy for an overactive imagination to come up with all manner of horrors and nameless fears.

In response to those fears, in his grace and compassion, our Heavenly Father allows us to practise what it is like to die faithfully, to die as a believer and follower of Christ, every single night of our lives. You know precisely what it feels like to die in Christ; it's like falling asleep. I have tried to imagine that feeling of being exhausted and drained after a long and gruelling day and then, at long last, your head touches the soft pillow. And all you have to do is give way to sleep, because you know you are safe, secure and protected. Falling asleep is not something strange or terrifying. It is an experience that our Heavenly Father gives us in advance so that we need not be fearful."

Barbara loved Shakespeare and taught Macbeth at A level. One of her favourite quotations from the play is in Act 2 scene 2,

"Sleep that knits up the ravelled sleeve of care,

The death of each day's life, sore labour's bath,
Balm of hurt minds, great nature's second course.
Chief nourisher in life's feast."

I think she loved that speech because it described how she felt about sleep. She loved to sleep and would take great pleasure in settling down for the night. But the true joy of a good night of sleep is awakening refreshed, soothed and healed - ready for a new day. In Psalm 17:15 the Psalmist speaks of his happiness in his ultimate awakening,

"As for me I shall behold your face in righteousness; I shall be satisfied when I awake in your likeness."

After the sleep of death, we will awake refreshed to see His face with its smile of welcome and we will know we are Home.

What is life without my love?

The pain of loss remains ever present and sometimes, stabs deeply. Yet it is not comfortless because we can picture our loved one in the perfect peace and joy of Home, where we too will join them when we open our eyes in that new and glorious world; satisfied to awake in His likeness.

For Reflection

Do you find the idea of going home at the end of life's journey a comfort?

Can you picture your loved one there awaiting your arrival?

Belief in 'afterlife' is a persistent reality in the humans heart. How do you imagine it?

David Winter in his book At the End of the Day mentions receiving a text from a woman who was dying in hospital who said, "Dying is really exciting!" She had great faith in the future. Not everyone would use those words to describe approaching death but is it possible to feel a sense of joyous anticipation at the end of life's day?

When the Sadducees came to trip Jesus up with their questions they laid out a far-fetched scenario. A woman's husband died, so as tradition dictated, his brother married her. There were seven brothers, they all died shortly after marrying her. So the facetious question was, "Whose wife will she be hereafter because she had been married to all seven?" Jesus replied, "You are mistaken because you don't know the scriptures or the power of God. For when the dead rise they will neither marry nor be given in marriage. They will be like the angels in heaven."

There is a sense of unbroken continuity but in a totally new and transformed dimension of existence.

Is that an inspiring vision and does the thought that your loved one is already there a source of comfort to you?

BIBLIOGRAPHY

Captain Corelli's Mandlin by Louis de Bernieres   Decker & Warburg 1994.

On Death and Dying by Elizabeth Kubler-Ross 1969 and 2008 Blockwell.

Bertrand Russell Autobiography 2010 Blackwell.

Fear no Evil by David Watson 1984 Hodder.

The Unutterable Beauty by G A Studdert-Kennedy originally published in 1927. Recent publishers, Meadow 2006.

Spiritual Care of Dying and Bereaved People by Penelope Wilcock BRF 2013

When Faith Gets Shaken by Patrick Regan   Eden 2018.

ABOUT THE AUTHOR

Rev Ian Jennings M.A. was Team Rector of Aston cum Aughton with Ulley and Swallownest in the Dicocese of Sheffield and he retired at Easter 2015. That coincided with a diagnosis of brain cancer for his wife Barbara. The following eighteen months were spent caring for her during her final illness. Ian's first book, *By a Departing Light,* was written following Barbara's death and, incidentally, at her suggestion. When they were told that Barbara's condition was terminal she said, "You must write a book about this." Ian felt that she instinctively knew that this would be a therapeutic exercise for him as well as offering some help to people in similar circumstances.

This book, *What is Life Without My Love?,* is more than a follow up, it tells the story of many who have who have also been thrust into this journey of grief and loss but who have found purpose and hope. There is so much to learn from their wisdom and experience. As Doctor Andrew Davies says, "This book will be a great consolation to many facing personal tragedy."

Ian was married to Barbara for 44 years and has been engaged in Christian Ministry for over 50 years. He is currently serving as Associate Minister at St. Mary's Denham. He said, "After Barbara's death I needed to be busy again and it is a joy to be part of a visionary parish with a great team of leaders."

He has two children, Paul who is married to Katie and is a Wing Commander in the Royal Air Force and Sarah who is a Mental Health Nurse. He has three grandsons, Joseph, Jamie, and George, who are a great source of joy.

If you have enjoyed this book, please do take a look at my other book **"By a Departing Light"** by visiting this link: **http://geni.us/departinglight**.

Printed in Poland
by Amazon Fulfillment
Poland Sp. z o.o., Wrocław